FISHING
THE LOCAL
WATERS
(West Palm Beach to Miami)

Second Edition

Also available from Maximum Press...

Fishing The Local Waters: (Gulf Shores to Panama City, third edition), Hoskins

FISHING
THE LOCAL
WATERS
(West Palm Beach to Miami)

Second Edition

Jim Hoskins
Illustrated by Valorie Langan and Ed Ilano

Maximum Press
605 Silverthorn Road
Gulf Breeze, Florida 32561
(904) 934-0819

Publisher: Jim Hoskins
Managing Editor: Brett Ledbetter
Editorial Production and Design: Type-Write Publications

Printed in the United States of America

10 9 8 7 6 5 4 3 2 1

To Monica ... my best fishing buddy,
To Nikolas ... my future fishing buddy,
and
To my parents ... who first taught me to fish

Acknowledgments

Many people assisted with the development of this book. Some provided valuable input; others reviewed the contents for accuracy and completeness. To those who helped, I thank you. I would especially like to thank Katie Bell, Dave Garland, Charles Griggs, Ruth Hoskins, Ray McAllister, Ray McConnell, Tim Murphy, and Bob Shipp.

Disclaimer

Fishing laws are subject to change without notice. Local authorities should always be consulted by the reader to ensure a complete understanding of current laws.

While some local boating safety information is provided in this book, it is not intended to replace safe boating publications or classes provided by the U. S. Coast Guard. This book assumes that the boater understands basic boating safety. All navigational information contained in this book is for reference only. Use only current U.S. Coast Guard charts and "Local Notice To Mariners" publications for navigation. Some LORAN coordinates contained in this book have not been verified.

Finally, sea conditions and currents can turn normally safe swimming areas into treacherous waters. Swimming is recommended only in lifeguard protected areas.

As a result of the foregoing, the author assumes no liability whatsoever for the continued accuracy of the information contained herein and disclaims any and all warranties, expressed or implied, as to the accuracy of said information.

Contents

Introduction

What This Book Is

Nothing is more frustrating than arriving in a new city, fishing rod in hand, and not knowing the details about fishing in the area. Even where the fishing is excellent, as it is in the waters around the Gold Coast (i.e., Palm Beach to Miami), an experienced fisherman can come away empty handed if he's not equipped with local fishing information. You need the answers to many questions such as, "Where, exactly, are the best fishing spots?"; "What kind of bait should I use?"; and, "What type of rigs and techniques are most effective on the local fish?" Fishing the Gold Coast is very different from fishing inland lakes or even fishing Florida's Gulf Coast. In each of these cases the kinds of fish are different, as are the types of baits, rigs, and techniques that are most effective.

That's just where this book comes in. It is a complete guide to saltwater fishing in the fertile waters of the Gold Coast. It provides information on some proven fishing spots, bait, and techniques. Fishing from shore is covered as well as fishing from a boat. The types of fish you are likely to catch are discussed, and fish identification charts are provided to help you sort out the good eating fish from the rest. Also included is a collection of Florida seafood recipes that are favorites in the area.

Whether you just want to spend a lazy afternoon fishing from shore or go on a full-scale boating excursion into the Atlantic, this book will equip you with the knowledge necessary to waste less time and catch more fish.

What This Book Is Not

Many fishing books try to be all things to all people. They start by explaining fly casting in mountain streams and finish by covering marlin fishing in Mexico. While these books are interesting, they do not provide information specific to a local area. They therefore leave many unanswered questions: "Exactly where do I go?"; "Which rigs, baits, and techniques should I use when I get there?"; and so on.

This book is not a general overview of fishing. It is specific to saltwater fishing locations, rigs, baits, and techniques proven to be productive in the waters from Palm Beach to Miami (a more than broad enough subject for a single book). This book will not teach you how to catch salmon off of Alaska nor will it get you ready for fishing the lakes in Canada. It will, instead, teach you — step by step — how to catch fish in the local waters around the Gold Coast.

How to Use This Book

Chapter 1 discusses the tackle, rigs, bait, and techniques used to fish the local inland waters. Bottom fishing, slip-rig fishing, and dealing with live shrimp are discussed. Popular inland fishing locations are listed and described, as are the types of fish you are likely to catch.

Chapter 2 discusses the tackle, rigs, bait, and techniques used to fish the Atlantic waters from the beach, jetties, or piers. Techniques for catching live bait are explained as are several effective fishing methods. Popular Atlantic fishing spots are listed and described. Fish typically caught in these areas are described.

Chapter 3 discusses the tackle, rigs, bait, and techniques used to fish the Atlantic waters from a boat. The types of fish caught by offshore Atlantic fishermen are discussed. Trolling, bottom fishing, drift fishing, and cast fishing are covered. LORAN C Lines of Position are given to many Atlantic fishing spots accessible by boat. Some local boating safety information is also provided.

Chapter 4 covers a variety of recipes available for the fish you catch using the pointers in this book. These recipes are taken from local favorites, and are both easy and delicious. A very nice ending to your fishing trip in the Gold Coast area.

Appendix A, "Fish Identification Charts" provides sketches of many fish commonly caught in the local waters. These can help you identify the fish you catch.

Appendix B, "Area Maps" contains the local maps that pinpoint the fishing spots discussed in this book.

"The Fisherman's Directory" at the back of this book is an alphabetical listing of many local merchants that cater to fishermen.

Environmentally Friendly Fishing

Fishing can be both relaxing and exciting. And nothing tastes better than freshly caught and well-prepared fish. While you are fishing, please help preserve the fishery and environment for those who follow both tomorrow and in years to come. We do not inherit the fishery from our parents; we borrow it from our children.

Here are some tips to help preserve the marine fishery and the environment:

*Please throw back any fish you don't want to eat or mount. Bring your camera and take pictures of the fish before you throw them back; photos make great trophies. Handle the fish gently and with wet hands.

*Please follow the bag limit laws. State and federal laws have been passed to prevent overfishing of various species. It is important to the long-term vitality of our waters that these laws be obeyed. The Florida Marine Patrol and the Alabama Marine Police actively enforce these laws, many of which carry heavy fines for violations.

*Please report any violation of marine fishery laws. You can do this by calling the Resource Alert line: (800) DIAL-FMP.

*Please pick up any floating garbage. You can make a difference and perhaps save the lives of marine creatures by simply picking up any floating garbage you may come across. Sea birds, turtles, and fish can eat or become entangled in the garbage. Besides, who want to see garbage floating around? Of course, don't throw any garbage (including cigarette butts) into the water.

Chapter

1

Fishing the Inland Waters

The **inland waters** around the Gold Coast offer convenient, inexpensive fishing that can be both relaxing and rewarding. For the purposes of this book, inland waters include the intracoastal waterways between the the Gold Coast beaches and the mainland as well as Biscayne Bay. For the boater, the inland waters are protected from winds, making for smoother waters and added safety as compared to the Atlantic Ocean. For those without a boat, the many sites listed in this chapter provide good fishing access to these waters. This chapter will survey some commonly caught fish and provide proven locations, baits, rigs, and techniques for fishing the inland waters of the Gold Coast.

What You Are Likely to Catch

While fishing the inland waters, you can catch many good eating fish. Some of the most common catches are listed in Figure 1-1.

Baits/Rigs/Techniques

Almost any type of fishing rod and reel can be used to fish the inland waters with any of the techniques described in this chapter. The weight of the tackle used (i.e., rod stiffness, line strength, reel size, etc.) is a

Type	Eating Quality	Active Periods	Typical Size (lbs.)
Black Drum	Fair	Spring	10–20 lb
Croaker	Good	Winter	1–2 lb
Jack Crevalle	Poor	All Year	5–20 lb
Mangrove Snapper	Excellent	Summer	1 lb
Sand Perch (Mojarra)	Excellent	Spring/Summer	½–2 lb
Sheepshead	Fair	Spring/Summer	2–5 lb
Snook	Excellent	Spring/Fall	10–12 lb
Tarpon	Poor	Summer	30–50 lb
Yellow tail (Snapper)	Excellent	All Year	1–5 lb

Figure 1-1: Fish commonly caught in the inland waters. See "Appendix A: Fish Identification Charts" for drawings of these fish.

matter of personal choice. Lightweight tackle (e.g. light action rod, closed-face reel, 10 lb test line) as shown in Figure 1-2 will test the fisherman's skill, allowing even the smaller fish to put up an interesting fight.

Heavier weight tackle (e.g., medium action rod, medium open face reel, 20 lb test line) as shown in Figure 1-3 will allow you to land a fish more quickly and will also allow easier handling of the bigger fish should you be particularly lucky.

After you have a rod and reel picked out, you must decide how you would like to fish. Two productive methods for fishing the local inland

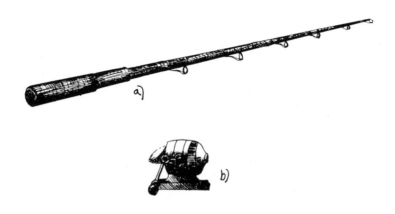

Figure 1-2: Light tackle suitable for inland water fishing.
a) Closed face reel. (b) Casting rod.

waters include:

* Slip-rig fishing
* Fishing with live shrimp

Slip-rig Fishing

A common form of fishing the local inland waters is slip-rig fishing. The baits most often used include **shrimp** or cut **mullet** (a local fish). Sand perch, black drum, and croakers are often caught with this technique. Figure 1-4 shows a slip-rig that can be used with any of these bait types.

This rig consists of a 2 or 3 oz egg weight, a 1/0 single hook, and a short leader with a swivel on one end and a clip on the other. There are several variations on the slip-rig available in any tackle shop, and most will produce about the same results. Most like simple leaders made of 30 to 50 lb test monofiliment line (a translucent plastic strand) rather than steel, since they are less visible to the fish. The single hook complies with laws restricting the use of multi-pronged hooks when fishing for some species. A 1/0 or 2/0 hook is large enough for most fish you are likely to encounter and small enough to be bite-size. The hooks are attached to the pre-made leader through a clip that is much like a safety pin. The egg weight, named after its shape, is designed to hold your bait on the bottom without getting snagged in the many oyster beds in the area. The egg weight is threaded on your fishing line before you tie on the leader. Your line is able too freely slide through the egg weight preventing a fish from feeling resistance when nibbling on your bait. A 2 or 3 oz egg weight will suit most situations providing a good casting weight while not overloading your rod. If you find your line is drifting to freely with the current, try going to a 3 or 4 oz egg weight.

The swivel used at the top of the leader prevents the egg weight from sliding down to the hook and also provides a place to tie on the fishing line. The knot used to tie the leader onto your fishing line is very important. An improper knot

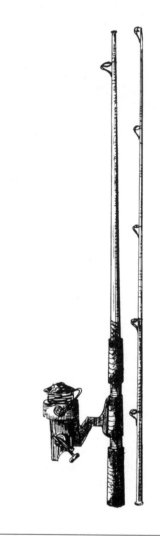

Figure 1-3: Medium-weight tackle suitable for inland water fishing.

can excessively weaken the line causing the line to break under the load of a fish. The Fisherman's knot is easy to tie and can be used for tying any type of rig onto your fishing line no matter where or how you are fishing. Figure 1-5 shows how this knot is tied. With a little practice, you will be able to quickly tie this knot.

After you have the leader tied to the line, you are ready to bait your hooks. As mentioned earlier, the most commonly used baits include shrimp and cut mullet. Shrimp often gets better results than mullet but it is also more expensive and harder to keep on your hook. Cut mullet is tougher and can sometimes get fish biting when shrimp is not producing strikes.

Shrimp will stay on the hook better if they are fresh (i.e., never been frozen). Many bait shops in the area sell fresh shrimp. Alternatively, frozen shrimp can be thawed under running tap water and used. In either case, remove the shrimp head and peel the shell off of the tail. Thread the hook through the shrimp tail as many times as possible. Threading the hook through the shrimp several times will make it more difficult for the fish to steal your bait. However, make sure the barb of the hook is visible when you are done. This makes it easier to hook the fish when he bites.

Figure 1-4: Slip-rig commonly used for fishing the inland waters.

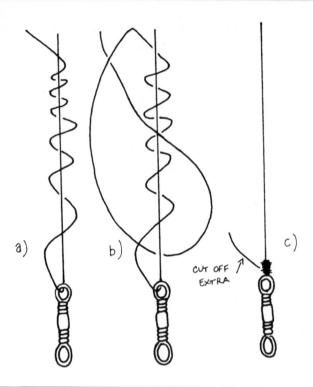

CUT OFF
EXTRA

Figure 1-5: Tying the Fisherman's knot. (a) First feed the line through the swivel part of the leader. Then wrap the loose end of the line around itself five to seven times. (b) Feed the end of the line through the loop created near the swivel and then back through the second loop just created. (c) Then gently pull on the line and the knot will draw down to the swivel. Cut off any excess line to complete the knot.

Mullet is an inexpensive fish that can be cut up for bait. To use mullet, cut strips from the body of the fish about 1/2 inch wide and 4 inches long. Thread the hook through the flesh several times. As always, make sure the barbs are visible after baiting the hook.

When your hooks are baited, cast the line into the water and allow it to sink completely to the bottom. Slack will develop in the line when the weight hits the bottom. Quickly retrieve any slack in the line and make it just taut, being careful not to slide the weight along the bottom. Usually, you will not have to wait long for bites. When you feel either steady tugging or one pronounced tug, snatch the rod tip towards the sky with a strong upward motion and wind the reel. When bringing in the fish, take care to keep the slack out of the line or you could lose it. As always, be sure and release any fish you don't want to eat.

Fishing with Live Shrimp

Usually, live shrimp will provide better results than dead baits because of the movements made by the shrimp as well as its more natural smell and taste. Snook are especially fond of live shrimp and can often be caught at night under the lights of a bridge. You can buy live shrimp by the dozen at local bait stores, and then it's your job to keep them from turning into dead shrimp. A styrofoam ice chest or a bait bucket filled with saltwater can be used to keep the shrimp alive. In either case, try to keep the shrimp in the shade to prevent the water from getting too hot, which will quickly kill the shrimp. Periodically scoop up some fresh salt water with another container and pour it into the live shrimp container. This will help keep them alive. Alternately, oxygen tablets or air pumps can also be used to extend the life of the shrimp.

The slip-rig technique described in the last section can be used with live shrimp. However, it's better to use a lighter weight to keep from slapping the shrimp too hard on the water's surface when casting. With live shrimp, switch to a 1 oz egg weight or even two small split-shot weights in place of the egg weight. Hook the live shrimp once through the head, being careful not to puncture the dark spot in the center of the head, which will kill the shrimp. This will allow the shrimp to move more freely, which, along with its fresh smell, will tantalize fish more than dead shrimp.

Where to Go

There are many places that provide inland water fishing access. Just about anywhere you can make a cast and hit the water has the potential of yielding fish. Water deeper than 10 feet near underwater structures is usually best. The spots described below are proven to be top fishing spots and can be reached by car or by boat.

#I1 - Little Blue Heron Bridge (Palm Beach)

Small bridge just east of Rivera Bridge provides good fishing. Occasional Spanish mackerel caught here. (Note: Fishing from Rivera Bridge is prohibited).

#I2 - Flagler Bridge (Palm Beach)

Very good fishing. Since this is a longer bridge, it is a good idea to have a bridge gaff when fishing here. Tarpon are caught here. Watch the traffic.

#I3 - Royal Park Bridge (Palm Beach)

This bridge, shown in Figure 1-6, is an active four-lane bridge with a step-up walkway on a centrally located main artery between West Palm Beach and Palm Beach. Watch the traffic while fishing.

#I4 - Old Lake Worth Bridge (Lake Worth)

Inactive bridge just north of the active Lake Worth Bridge. Half of the old bridge is open for fishing. Bluefish occasionally caught here. Fishing from the active Lake Worth Bridge is prohibited.

Figure 1-6: The Royal Park Bridge in Palm Beach offers good fishing access to the Intracoastal Waterway. However, traffic is usually heavy, so be careful.

#I5 - Lantana Bridge (Lantana)

Active bridge over the Intracoastal Waterway at Ocean Avenue. Good for sand perch and others. Watch the traffic.

#I6 - C-15 Locks (Boca Raton)

Used to control flooding, the C-15 Locks are an excellent place to catch snook and tarpon. Here, you walk down to the lock and fish along the shore near the outfall from the lock.

#I7 - *Under Spanish River Bridge (Boca Raton)*

Area under Spanish River Bridge provides parking and fishing access to the Intracoastal Waterway.

#I8 - *Palmetto Park Bridge (Boca Raton)*

Active two-lane bridge along over the Intracoastal Waterway. Cement step-up walkway provided. This is a low bridge, thus providing good fishing access.

#I9 - *A1A Bridge (Boca Raton)*

Active two-lane bridge over the narrow canal leading to the Boca Raton inlet. Cement step-up walkway provided. Proximity to the Atlantic provides a chance to catch some stray Atlantic species.

#I10 - *Camino Real Bridge (Boca Raton)*

Active two-lane bridge over the Intracoastal Waterway. Cement step-up walkway provided. Also a low bridge providing good fishing access.

#I11 - *Hillsboro Bridge (Pompano Beach)*

Active two-lane bridge over the narrow canal leading to the Hillsboro inlet. Cement step-up walkway provided. Proximity to the Atlantic provides a chance to catch some stray Atlantic species.

#I12 - Atlantic Blvd. Bridge (Pompano Beach)

Active bridge over the Intracoastal Waterway.

#I13 - Commercial Blvd. Bridge (Lauderdale by the Sea)

Active bridge over the Intracoastal. Good for snapper and sheepshead among other things. Watch the traffic.

#I14 - Oakland Park Beach Bridge (Ft. Lauderdale)

Active bridge over the Intracoastal. Occasional tarpon caught here. Watch the traffic.

#I15 - Dania Beach Blvd. Bridge (Hollywood)

Active bridge over the Intracoastal. Good for snapper and snook.

#I16 - Sheridan Street Bridge (Hollywood)

Active bridge over the Intracoastal.

#I17 - Hallendale Beach Blvd. Bridge (Hallendale)

Active bridge over the Intracoastal.

#I18 - Broad Causeway (North Miami)

Active bridge over the Intracoastal.

#I19 - Old Rickenbacker Causeway Bridge (Miami)

This popular fishing spot, shown in Figure 1-7, is an inactive bridge next to the active Rickenbacker Causeway Bridge. It provides good fishing access to Biscayne Bay. Good parking on either side of bridge. Walk out and fish. Benches and garbage cans are provided. No fishing from active Rickenbacker Causeway Bridge.

Figure 1-7: The Old Rickenbacker Causeway Bridge in Miami offers excellent fishing access to the waters of Biscayne Bay.

#120 - Cape Florida State Recreation Area (Key Biscayne)

A sea wall, shown in Figure 1-8, provides good fishing access to Biscayne Bay. The sea wall is located in the southwestern section of the Cape Florida State Recreation Area. There is a picnic area with rest rooms adjacent to the sea wall, and ample parking is available. An Atlantic beach for swimming, a historic lighthouse, and concessions are located elsewhere in the park. There is a fee for entry into the park.

Figure 1-8: The sea wall in Cape Florida State Recreation Area offers fishing access to Biscayne Bay and other activities for non-fishing members of your party.

Chapter

2

Fishing the Atlantic
from Shore/Piers

While the inland waters offer much good fishing, the Atlantic waters are also accessible to the shore-bound fisherman. The Atlantic offers a whole new set of fish to catch using some additional techniques. Fishing can be done from virtually any beach area or from one of the ocean piers or jetties.

What You Are Likely to Catch

The Atlantic Ocean offers many good-eating species of fish. The larger fish found in the Atlantic also make for excellent sport fishing for even the most seasoned anglers. Figure 2-1 lists some of the more common catches.

Baits/Rigs/Techniques

When fishing in the Atlantic, you have better chances of catching larger fish. As always though, almost any fishing tackle can be used to fish the Atlantic. The weight of the fishing tackle used is a matter of personal preference. Light tackle for the Atlantic might include a light action rod 6 feet length, a medium sized open face reel, and 15 lb test line similar to the setup shown in Figure 1-3. Heavier tackle for fishing the Atlantic from shore or from a pier might include a heavier action 8 foot rod, a

Type	Eating Quality	Active Periods	Typical Size (lbs.)
Barracuda	Poor	Summer	10–50 lb
Bluefish	Fair	Winter/Spring	2–20 lb
Bonito	Poor	Summer	4–20 lb
Cero Mackerel	Excellent	Summer	5–15 lb
Cobia	Excellent	Winter	10–50 lb
Jack Crevelle	Poor	All Year	5–20 lb
King Mackerel	Good	Winter/Summer/Spring	8–40 lb
Permit	Excellent	Summer	2–5 lb
Pompano	Excellent	Fall/Spring	2–5 lb
Sheepshead	Fair	Spring/Summer	2–5 lb
Snook	Excellent	Spring/Fall	10–12 lb
Spanish Mackerel	Excellent	Spring/Winter/Fall	2–15 lb
Whiting	Excellent	Winter	1–3 lb
Yellowtail (Snapper)	Excellent	All year	1–5 lb

Figure 2-1: Fish commonly caught in the Atlantic from shore/ piers. See "Appendix A: Fish Identification Charts" for drawings of these fish.

larger open face reel, and 25 lb test line. Since the larger fish in the Atlantic tend to run when hooked, make sure whatever reel you have is filled to capacity with line (but not over filled). For those fishing from the beach, a longer spinning rod (8 to 10 feet) and light 15 lb test line will increase your casting distance.

When fishing the Atlantic from a pier, you will find yourself some distance above the surface of the water. For this reason, you will have to lift the full weight of the fish you catch from the surface to pier level. Smaller fish can be brought up by grabbing the fishing line with gloved hands and pulling the fish up hand over hand. This is called hand-lining the fish. However, larger fish will often be too heavy to lift from the surface of the water with just your fishing line. For this reason, you should have access to a gaff when fishing from an Atlantic pier. The type of gaff typically used on a pier consists of a rope with a large grappling hook on the end which can be lowered to the water's surface, pulled into a fish, and used to bring the fish up to pier level. Most piers have a gaff available for public use, but you may want to keep a small one in your tackle box just in case.

There are several different techniques for Atlantic fishing from shore/piers — including surf fishing, cast fishing, and drift fishing. Let's take a look at the following techniques:

* Surf fishing
* Slip-rig fishing
* Balloon fishing
* Fishing with lures

Surf Fishing

Fishing directly from the beach without the benefit of a pier or jetty is known as surf fishing. Pompano, whiting, permit, and bluefish include species commonly caught surf fishing. The baits most commonly used include sand fleas, shrimp, and cut mullet (a local fish). Sand fleas look much like white egg weights with legs and are usually best. When they are around, you can catch them by digging in the sand right down at the water's edge as the waves recede.

Figure 2-2 shows a surf fishing rig that can be used with any of these bait types. This rig consists of a double drop leader, two 1/0 or 2/0 single hooks, and a 2 or 3 oz pyramid weight. The double drop leader allows you to offer two baits to the fish with every cast. Since fish are good at stealing the bait off of the hooks, two baits means they will have to work twice as hard to leave you empty handed. There are several variations on the double drop leader available in any tackle shop, but all will produce about the same results. Most like simple leaders made of heavy monofiliment line rather than steel, since they are less visible to the fish. However, steel leaders may be necessary when the bluefish are running. A 1/0 or 2/0 hook is large enough for most fish you are likely to encounter and small enough to be bite-size. The hooks are attached to the leader through clips that are much like safety pins. The pyramid weight, named after its shape, is designed to stick into the sand bottom like those in local waters providing more holding power against any currents. The pyramid weight is also attached to a safety-pin type clip on the very bottom of the leader. A 3 or 4 oz weight will suit most situations, providing a good casting weight while not overloading your rod.

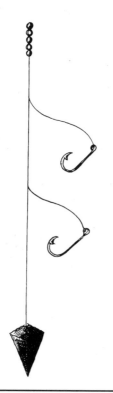

A swivel is usually provided at the top of the leader and is used as a place to tie on the fishing line and also to prevent line twisting by rotating as necessary. Use the Fishermen's knot described earlier to tie the leader onto your line. After you have the leader tied to the line, you are ready to bait your hooks. As mentioned earlier, the most commonly used baits include sand fleas, shrimp, and cut mullet. When using sand fleas, simply thread the hook through the sand flea's body one time making sure the barb of the hook is exposed. When sand

Figure 2-2: Rig commonly used for surf fishing in the Atlantic.

fleas are not available, shrimp is usually preferred over cut mullet. However, shrimp is more expensive and harder to keep on your hook. However, cut mullet can sometimes get fish biting when shrimp is not producing strikes. Hook shrimp or cut mullet strips onto the hooks using the method described in the last chapter under "Slip-rig fishing" in the last chapter.

When your hooks are baited, cast the line into the water and allow it to sink completely to the bottom. Slack will develop in the line when the weight hits the bottom. Quickly retrieve any slack in the line and make it just taut, being careful not to slide the weight along the bottom. Usually, you will not have to wait long for bites. When you feel either steady tugging or one pronounced tug, snatch the rod tip towards the sky with a strong upward motion and wind the reel. When bringing in the fish, take care to keep the slack out of the line or you could lose it. As always, be sure and release any fish you don't want to eat.

Slip-rig Fishing

Slip-rig fishing is commonly used when fishing from Atlantic piers and jetties. Atlantic slip-rig fishing techniques are exactly like those discussed in "Slip-rig fishing" in Chapter 1. However, to handle the larger fish of the Atlantic, heavier monofilament leader material (e.g., 40 or 50 lb test) is often used. These techniques when used in the Atlantic, can yield snook, bluefish, sheepshead, pompano, whiting, and others.

Balloon Fishing

The balloon fishing technique can yield excellent results with a variety of different baits. This technique is fairly simple and often yields king mackerel, Spanish mackerel, and bonito.

The rig used is shown in Figure 2-3. It consists of a length of steel leader material as long as the fish you intend to catch, a swivel used to tie the fishing line on and reduce line twisting, and a single hook. Based on the type of fish active, the leader material strength should be 40 lb test (Spanish mackerel) or 60 lb test (king mackerel). The heavier 60 lb test leader material is more visible underwater so that smaller Spanish mackerel may be leery. However, the 60 lb test leader strength is necessary if larger king mackerel are hitting. In general, it is best to use as little hardware as possible since this makes it harder for the fish to see the rig. A black swivel is less visible than a brass swivel and is therefore preferred. A #5 swivel is an appropriate size swivel for king mackerel or Spanish mackerel. A 5/0 single hook should be large enough for the job. Many times these rigs will be available pre-made at the tackle shop. Alternatively, you can buy the materials and make your own rigs. If you choose to make your own, you will first need leader material. The non-coated braided steel wire type (e.g., Sevenstrand® brand) is fairly easy to work with. You will also need a pair of sharp wire cutters to cleanly cut the leader material. Figure 2-4 shows how this rig is made.

Once you have your rig, tie it onto the line using the Fisherman's knot shown in Figure 1-5. With this type of fishing, you want the bait to be just a few feet below the surface. An ordinary balloon is an easy way to keep your bait fish near the surface and allow you to watch any action develop.

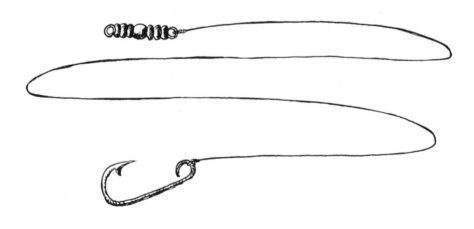

Figure 2-3: Rig used for balloon fishing in the Atlantic.

Simply blow up a balloon to about 5 inches in diameter and tie a knot to keep the air in. Then, with a second knot, tie the balloon around the fishing line about five feet above the hook. You are then ready to hook up a small bait fish. You can use a sardine, blue runner, goggle-eye, or some other small fish.

Frozen sardines are usually available in area tackle shops. They should be thawed out before use. Running warm water over them will accelerate this process if necessary. You want the sardine to look as natural as

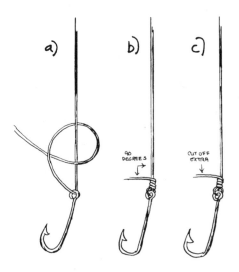

a)   b)   c)

90 DEGREES

CUT OFF EXTRA

Figure 2-4: First cut a length of leader material the length of the largest fish you expect to catch (36 to 48 inches is a good rule of thumb). Feed one end of the leader material through the eye of the hook and tie an overhand knot as shown in Figure 2-4 (a). Then, being careful to make a sharp 90 degree bend in the leader material, wrap the leader material around itself in a barrel twist (five to seven turns will be sufficient). It is critical that the material be wrapped around the leader material at 90 degrees as shown in (b). Now attach the swivel to the other end of the leader material using the same barrel twist technique.

possible, so gently move the body from side to side as if the fish were swimming to make the fish more flexible. Then hook the fish up under the jaw between the gill plates coming out of the top of the nose just in front of the eyes as shown in Figure 2-5 (a).

If you can get a live blue runner or goggle-eye, you are more likely to catch fish. However, due to the difficulties of keeping live bait fish, tackle shops don't usually sell them live. You will have to catch your own. You can do this with a slip-rig (discussed in Chapter 1) consisting of a 1/0 hook and a 1 oz egg weight. Bait the hook with a small amount of shrimp or cut bait. Cast the baited hook near the pilings of a pier or near the rocks of a jetty and see what you catch. If bait fish are around, you may be able to get a few live ones this way. Although blue runners and goggle-eyes are a top dinner choice among local fish, there is no "best bait" for all situations, so any kind of live bait fish may turn out to be better than fishing with dead sardines. To hook a live bait fish of any type, simply pass the hook through the back of the fish as shown in Figure 2-5 (b).

With your rig baited, you are now ready to drift fish. Before you begin to fish, you must set the reel's drag. The drag is designed to automatically dispense line as you are fighting a fish before the breaking point of the line is reached. This prevents a strong fish from breaking the line. The drag should be set to yield line well before the breaking point of the line is reached. Most fish caught using this technique will break the line if the drag is set too tight. If the drag is too loose, however, you will not be able to properly hook or fight the fish. A little experimenting is necessary to find the right setting.

Just give the bait fish a good cast down current and allow it to seek its own level. Leave the reel free spooled, meaning that line can freely flow off of the reel. With your fingers, prevent further line from being released by lightly hold the line with your fingers. **DO NOT WRAP THE LINE AROUND YOUR FINGER. IT COULD BE INJURED IF A LARGE FISH TAKES THE LINE.**

When a fish takes the bait, he will start to run pulling the line from your loose finger grip. The reel will then feed the fish line without any tension as you point the rod towards the fish. The fish's action will usually cause the balloon to pop so that it doesn't provide resistance when dragging through the water. At this point it is important to let the fish have line so that it doesn't feel any tension for a full count of four (one thousand one...one thousand two...etc.). This usually gives the fish time to swallow the bait. Once you have finished counting, quickly begin to wind the reel, which will stop the line from freely feeding out, and strongly snatch the rod tip up towards the sky several times. Continue to hold tension in the line at all times by keeping the rod tip up and constantly winding the reel, allowing the drag to determine your progress. After the hook is well set, stop winding but continue to hold the rod tip towards the sky. If the fish is running and pulling out line against your drag, let him go. This is what you want to happen. The fish is working very hard and will soon tire. Once the running stops, wind the reel as you slowly lower the tip of the rod towards the fish being careful not to give any slack in the line. When the rod tip is almost towards the fish, stop reeling and

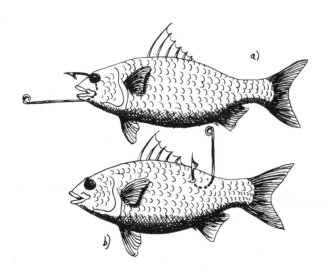

Figure 2-5: Hooking bait fish. (a) Hooking a dead bait fish.
(b) Hooking a live bait fish.

begin to pull the fish in by gently pulling the rod tip back towards the sky. Continue this pumping action (reeling the tip down and then pulling the tip back towards the sky) to work the fish towards you. Let the fish get fully exhausted and under your control before trying to land him. If you are on a pier and the fish is too large to lift without breaking your line, use a gaff (described earlier).

Fishing with Lures

An alternative to fishing with bait is to use lures or artificial bait. A lures commonly used when fishing from the Atlantic piers and jetties is shown in Figure 2-6. This lure, often called a "side winder" or "buck-tail" jig, can be used to catch Spanish mackerel and bluefish among others. Since both Spanish and bluefish have sharp teeth, a steel leader (e.g., 40 lb test) is recommended. You can purchase ready-made steel leaders that provide a swivel on one end and a clip for the lure on the other. Alternately, you can make your own leader by following the directions provided in the last section and substituting your lure for the hook.

Once you have the lure and leader ready, tie the leader's swivel onto your line using the fishermen's knot. Then cast the lure and allow it to settle for five seconds or so. As you wind the reel, start "working" the lure by making short and frequent jerks of your rod tip (about one jerk per second will work). When a fish hits, you will feel resistance to your jerk. Then sharply snatch your rod tip towards the sky several times to set the hook. As you fight your fish, be careful not to give any slack in the line which might allow the fish to get away. After you land your fish, simply unhook the lure and you are ready to catch another.

Where to Go

There are many fishing spots along the beaches of the Gold Coast that provide access to the Atlantic Ocean. Fishing in the surf line anywhere along the beach can provide good results using the surf fishing techniques described in this chapter. Pompano, permit, bluefish, and whiting are commonly caught bottom fishing from the beach in this manner. However, the wave action along the beach and the slow slopping bottom usually make balloon fishing from the beach difficult at best. The Atlantic piers and jetties provide good platforms for the slip-rig and balloon fishing techniques described in this chapter. King mackerel, Spanish mackerel, cobia, and so on, are more likely to be caught off of the Atlantic piers. Some of the prime fishing locations for fishing the Atlantic from piers and jetties are discussed below.

#A1 - Lake Worth Inlet North Jetty (Lake Worth)

Rock jetty bordering both sides of the Lake Worth Inlet. You can get to the jetty on the North side of the inlet by parking and walking down the beach. There is no public access to the jetty on the South side of the inlet.

#A2 - Lake Worth Municipal Pier (Lake Worth)

This pier, shown in Figure 2-7, is in the heart of Lake Worth. It is near a lifeguard protected beach, restaurants, shops, and a municipal pool. The many different activites available in the area make this a good choice when you have non-fishing members of your party. The pier itself is 940 feet long and claims to provide fishing closest to the waters of the Gulf Stream located a short distance off shore. An occasional sail fish is taken off of

Figure 2-6: Side winder/ bucktail

this pier due to its proximity to the Gulf Stream. Some benches are provided, and there are two sections of the pier covered by roof offering shade and protection from rain. There is a fee for fishing here.

#A3 - Boyton Inlet Jetty (Boyton Beach)

This jetty consists of cement structures, one on each side of the Boyton Inlet. The top of the structures is flat and a simple rail system provides something to hold onto. The waters run swiftly in this jetty and the waves often break over the wall (especially on the north side) when the Atlantic is rough. Absolutly no swimming in the inlet area! Either side provides good fishing access.

#A4 - Jap Rock (Boca Raton)

This spot is some large rocks that offer a fishing platform with access to the Atlantic. Park near Spanish River bridge and walk to the rocks. Good for snapper and an occasional barracuda.

#A5 - South Inlet Park (Boca Raton)

This jetty and beach area on the south side of the Boca Raton Inlet is shown in Figure 2-8. When conditions are right, the beach just to the south of the jetty provides good sunning and lifeguard protected swimming. There is also a picnic area with an ocean view in a wooded area just off of the beach. Good parking and restrooms with showers are provided. There is a fee for entry into the park.

#A6 - Deerfield Fishing Pier (Deerfield Beach)

This pier is in the heart of Deerfield Beach. It is on a lifeguard protected beach with resturaunts and shops. The diversity of activites available in

Figure 2-7: Lake Worth Fishing Pier.

the area make this a good choice when you have non-fishing members in your party. There is a fee for fishing here.

#A7 - Atlantic Pier (Pompano Beach)

This is a 1,080 foot pier in the heart of Pompano Beach. The pier is equipped with benches and tanks for live bait. A portion of the pier near the end is covered providing shade and shelter from rain. Resturants and shops are in the area. The pier is adjacent to a lifeguard protected beach area. There is a fee for fishing here.

#A8 - Port Everglades Jetties/State Park (Hollywood)

The John U. Lloyd Beach State Recreation Area is located on the south side of the entrance to Port Everglades. A jetty at the northern end of the

Figure 2-8: Jettie located in Boca Raton's South Inlet Park.

park provides excellent fishing access. A nearby beach area offers swiming and scuba diving on nearby reefs. Snacks, picnic supplies, boat ramps, and canoes are also available. Picnic areas are located along the beach front. There is a fee for entering the park. Alternately, the north side of the Port Everglades Jetties can provide fishing access. However, you must park and walk a half of a mile to get to the north jetty.

#A9 - Dania Pier (Hollywood)

This pier is in Hollywood at the end of Daina Beach Blvd. A portion of the pier near the end is covered providing shade and shelter from rain. Resturants and shops are in the area. The pier is adjacent to a lifeguard protected beach area. There is a fee for fishing here.

#A10 - Newport Fishing Pier (Miami Beach)

This privately owned pier is 350 feet long. It is located on Collins Avenue at 167th Street on Miami Beach. Benches and lights are provided on the pier as well as a covered section offering some shade and refuge from the rain. It is adjacent to lifeguard protected beaches. There is a fee for fishing here.

#A11 - Haulover Fishing Pier (Haulover Beach)

Figure 2-9 shows this pier, which is located just north of Bal Harbor. It is 1,103 feet long and is equipped with running water, benches, lights, a covered area, and two "T"'s providing much fishing space. It is adjacent to lifeguard protected beaches. While there aren't any shops in the area, there is a snack bar and tackle shop on the pier. There is a fee for fishing here.

Figure 2-9: Haulover Fishing Pier.

#A12 - Haulover Inlet Jetty (Haulover Beach)

The Bal Harbor inlet has jetties that provide good fishing access to the Atlantic. The south side of the jetty provides a smooth walkway out onto the jetty. Snook are frequently caught here. Located just south of the Haulover Fishing Pier.

#A13 - Government Cut Jetty (Miami Beach)

A wooden pier alongside a jetty at the south end of South Point Park provides excellent access to the Atlantic waters. It is located on the southern tip of Miami Beach. Picnic areas and a playground for children are also located within the park. There is a fee for park entry.

Chapter

3

Fishing the Atlantic from a Boat

With a boat, you have access to the best fishing the Gold Coast has to offer. While much good fishing can be had from shore, a boat offers access to deeper water and underwater structures that attract bait fish and their inevitable predators. There are some natural reef structures as well as artificial reefs (sunken ships, rubble, etc.) within easy reach for the boater. Before we get into fishing the Atlantic from a boat, let's pause to cover some safety information.

Local Boating Safety Information

The Atlantic offers clear, warm, and usually calm waters that can provide many days of safe boating and excellent fishing. As with boating anywhere, though, safety is of primary importance. The U.S. Coast Guard offers safe boating classes all over the country that will help teach you basic boating safety. The classes are highly recommended either as an introduction to new boaters or as a refresher for old salts.

In addition, safe boating requires knowledge about the local area in which you intend to operate. While complete boating safety information is beyond the scope of this book, here are some safety tips related to the area.

Weather Patterns

The weather around the Gold Coast is often difficult to predict. Especially in the summer, thunderstorms are common and can quickly develop, catching boaters by surprise. For this reason, boaters should frequently check the weather reports that are broadcast 24 hours a day on VHF radio channels 1, 2, and 3. What appears to be a sunny calm day can quickly become filled with intense localized thunderstorms spawning water spouts. As always, use good judgement. Know where you are in relation to the closest pass at all times, and don't venture beyond the safe range of your boat or experience. For smaller boats, there is plenty of good fishing in inland waters and in the Atlantic waters immediately around passes.

Since the summers in this area are both hot and humid, be sure and keep plenty of water on board. A good way to do this is to take plastic milk jugs, fill them with water and freeze them the night before the trip. You can use these frozen jugs in ice chests to keep your fish/food cool while having reserve water when they thaw. Another necessity for spending a day in the Atlantic (or inland waters for that matter) is shade. The hot sun will quickly overheat an unprotected fishermen as well as produce intense sunburns. Even a simple Bimini top can provide the refuge from the sun necessary for spending extended periods on a boat. However, don't underestimate the effects of sun rays reflected off of the water. These rays can burn exposed skin and eyes even while you are in the shade! Invest in some potent sun blocking lotion, sunglasses (polarized sunglasses will let you see into the water better), and a hat with a bill.

While fishing is still good (and sometimes better) in the winter, frequent north winds often make the Atlantic waters rough. In other words, there are fewer calm days in the winter than in the summer. Further, the cold winds can quickly chill an exposed fisherman, especially when dampened by 60 degree sea spray. For these reasons, winter boating typically requires a larger boat than summer boating to handle the larger seas and provide protection from the cold.

Inlets

Inland waters provide access to the Atlantic mostly through narrow channels cut through the barrier island. Strong currents are frequently found in these areas, as large quantities of water are shifting due to tidal actions. These strong currents along with tidal actions constantly shift the bottom profiles in these areas, often creating new shallow areas that weren't there the week before. These shallow areas along with tidal currents present in inlets can make even small waves very dangerous for boating. Small boats are swamped and capsized almost every year trying to get through the inlets in less than ideal conditions. If you are not familiar with navigating a particular inlet, you may want to stick with inland water fishing or at least watch a few other boats go through the pass before deciding whether or not to proceed.

Diver Down Flags

Skin and SCUBA divers are required by law to display a diver down flag while diving. There are two types of diver down flags. One is a red square with a white diagonal stripe; the other is a blue and white "V" shaped flag.

When you see a diver down flag, reduce your speed and exercise extreme caution, as surfacing divers may be difficult to see in the water.

What if You Have Boat Trouble?

Every year there are boaters that find themselves stranded in the Atlantic needing assistance. These boaters might have engine failures, electrical failures, or might have simply run out of gas. In any case, the U.S. Coast Guard is ever ready to provide assistance.

If you find yourself stranded in the Atlantic, first anchor your vessel if possible to prevent drifting further from shore, to more isolated areas, or into breaking surf. Then try to contact the Coast Guard on VHF Channel 16. This channel is to be used exclusively for distress calls or hailing other vessels. Messages like "Coast Guard Station... this is the (name of your vessel) over ...." The Coast Guard will respond asking you to switch to another channel (probably Coast Guard working VHF channels 21, 23, or 81). They will want information like your position, the nature of your distress, the number of people on board, and so on. If necessary, they will dispatch a Coast Guard vessel or contact a towing service in order to tow you to a nearby port.

While a VHF radio is strongly recommended anytime you venture into the Atlantic, electrical failures can render them useless. Some boaters carry a spare hand-held VHF radio as a back-up. If you are unable to communicate via radio for whatever reason, you should try to flag down any vessels in the area by waving a bright rag or shirt and sounding your horn, bell, or whistle. The other vessel may be able to tow you into port or call the Coast Guard for you. If you are unable to hail another vessel, your last resort is to fire off flares to attract attention. Anytime you are stranded in the Atlantic, the situation should be taken seriously and action should be taken promptly.

What You Are Likely to Catch

When fishing from a boat, you have the added advantage of reaching deeper water and various underwater structures that are home to many large and good eating fish. Figure 3-1 lists some of the more common catches.

Baits/Rigs/Techniques

A boat is an excellent platform for a variety of fishing techniques. Since there are more large fish found in the deeper Atlantic waters accessible by boat, heavier fishing tackle is usually in order. Due to the flexibility offered by boat fishing, more decisions have to be made as to the type of fishing you want to do. While the same tackle can be used for most any type of fishing, some equipment is better suited to a particular technique

Type	Eating Quality	Active Periods	Typical Size (lbs.)
Amberjack	Excellent	All Year	5–50 lb
Barracuda	Poor	Summer	10–50 lb
Bluefish	Fair	Winter/Spring	2–20 lb
Bonito	Poor	Summer	4–20 lb
Cero Mackerel	Excellent	Summer	5–15 lb
Cobia	Excellent	Winter	10–50 lb
Dolphin	Excellent	Spring/Summer/Fall	2–40 lb
Grouper	Excellent	All Year	2–30 lb
King mackerel	Good	Winter/Summer/Spring	8–40 lb
Red snapper	Excellent	All Year	2–8 lb
Sheepshead	Fair	Spring/Summer	2–5 lb
Snook	Excellent	Spring/Fall	10–12 lb
Spanish Mackerel	Excellent	Spring/Winter/Fall	2–15 lb
Triggerfish	Excellent	All Year	2–5 lb
Yellowtail Snapper	Excellent	All year	1–5 lb

Figure 3-1: Fish commonly caught in the Atlantic while fishing from a boat. See "Appendix A: Fish Identification Charts" for drawings of these fish.

than another. Additional equipment necessary for the boating Atlantic fisherman is a hand gaff and fishing gloves. The gaff used from a boat consists of a handle or pole with a large hook attached to the end. This gaff is used to lift an exhausted fish from the surface of the water and into your boat. Without a gaff, you would have to hand-line the fish into the boat by grabbing the fishing line with gloved hands and pulling. For larger fish, this could result in pulling out the hook or breaking the line, either of which will lose the fish for you. The fishing gloves help protect your hands from line burns, sharp fins, and so on.

Landing a large fish is a two person operation. As the fisherman works the exhausted fish towards the boat, the gaffer puts on his work gloves to protect his hands. Then the gaffer grabs the fishing line loosely with one hand and pulls the fish into reach. With the other hand, he positions the gaff hook under the fish. With one smooth motion, he pulls the gaff up and into the fish's midsection, continuing to lift the gaff and fish directly into the boat.

Many Atlantic fish (e.g. king mackerel) have very sharp teeth which can inflict a nasty bite. **NEVER PUT YOUR HANDS INTO A FISH'S MOUTH FOR ANY REASON!** Even after a fish has been out of the water for a good while and appears to be motionless, he may still have enough life left to suddenly snap his jaws. Use pliers and gloves when removing hooks from the fish's mouth.

With this understanding, let's examine the following fishing techniques that are known to be productive when fishing the Gulf by boat:

* Bottom fishing
* Trolling
* Drift fishing

Bottom Fishing

Of all the techniques discussed in this section, bottom fishing is the most reliable way to ensure you don't come back empty handed. This along with the fact that it is also one of the simplest techniques to learn makes it a good place for the beginner to start. The local favorites red snapper, grouper, and amberjack are caught using this technique. The most important thing when bottom fishing in the Atlantic is to make sure you are over some type of irregularity in the bottom such as a ship wreck, a ledge, rocks, and so on. These types of underwater irregularities provide a platform for the growth of underwater organisms which provide food for small baitfish. As these baitfish collect, they attract larger fish which feed on the baitfish. Since most of the Atlantic bottom is barren sand, randomly anchoring over any old spot is a sure way to decrease your odds of catching fish when bottom fishing. The section entitled "Where to Go" later in this chapter will help you anchor on a good spot.

While most any type of tackle can be used, the larger fish you are likely to encounter while bottom fishing the Atlantic will require heavy tackle. You will be fishing near ship wrecks, rock piles, and so on, and the bottom fish who live here are very good at entangling your line once they are hooked. When a fish is hooked, it is a natural reaction for it to swim frantically through the wreck or structure seeking safety and dragging your fishing line with him. Nothing is more frustrating than finally hooking the "big one" only to have your line quickly cut by a piece of scrap metal on the bottom.

The way to avoid this problem is to pull the fish off of the bottom as quickly as you can. Especially for larger bottom fish, this requires a heavy rod, heavy line, and a strong reel, all designed for bottom fishing, like the tackle shown in Figure 3-2.

The type of rig used for this type of bottom fishing is shown in Figure 3-3. Since many bottom fish (especially red snapper and grouper) can see quite well, it is important to make the rig as invisible as possible. For this reason, heavy monofilament line (not steel leader material) is used to make the rig.

Tackle stores sell similar rigs ready made, or you can make your own with a little practice. To make the rigs, you will first need a spool of 60 lb test monofiliment line. Figure 3-4 shows how to make a bottom rig. After you have made a few bottom rigs, you will be able to make them very quickly. Now tie the swivel on your rig on to your line using the Fisherman's knot and you are ready to fish.

The bait used for bottom fishing in the Atlantic includes sardines (sometimes cut into halves or thirds), shrimp, squid, or other cut bait. In any case, put the point of the hook through the bait at least two times and make sure that the barb is exposed. Then lower the baited rig down to the bottom and then wind up two turns of the reel. Point the rod tip down towards the water and wait. When you feel a strike, snatch the rod up towards the sky and begin to wind the reel. If you have hooked the fish, pull him a few feet off of the bottom as quickly as possible to avoid becoming entangled or cut off. Then allow the fish to tire as you consistently work him towards the surface. When the fish reaches the surface, he can be hand-lined or gaffed as necessary.

When fishing the deeper Atlantic waters (around 80 feet deep and deeper) where large grouper and other fish are found, a large slip-rig (Figure 3-5) is often used. Since grouper can also be "spooked" by steel leader material, heavy monofilament line is used.

Again, this rig may be purchased or easily made. First, cut a length of 60 or 80 lb test monofilament line 48 to 60 inches long. Using the Fisherman's knot (but with only four or five turns), tie a #5 swivel on one end and a 3/0 hook on the other. Thread your fishing line through an egg weight (4 to 8 oz) and then tie your line to the swivel using the Fisherman's knot.

With this rig, a whole baitfish is used. Dead sardines are hooked through the nose while live bait fish (blue runners or goggle-eyes) are hooked through the tail (see Figure 2-5) Since the line freely feeds through the egg weight, this rig lets larger fish take line without feeling the weight, giving them time to swallow the bait fish.

After you bait the rig, make sure the drag is set such that the reel will give line before the breaking point is reached. Now lower the rig to the bottom slowly to avoid getting the rig twisted around itself. Once on the bottom, leave the reel disengaged and stop line from running off of the reel by resting your thumb on the line. Now you wait.

When a fish takes the bait, feed him line for a full count of five (one

a)

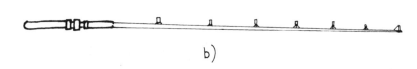

b)

Figure 3-2: Heavyweight tackle used for bottom fishing in the Atlantic.

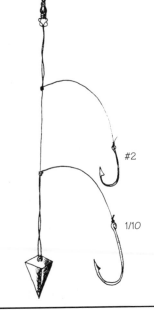

#2

1/10

thousand one ... one thousand two ... etc.). Then lock the reel, snatch the rod towards the sky, and reel. Try to get the fish a few feet off of the bottom as quickly as possible to avoid having your line cut on any bottom structures. Once you are some distance off of the bottom, allow the fish to tire before bringing him to the surface. Then, depending on the size of the fish, either hand-line the fish into the boat or gaff it.

Figure 3-3: Bottom rig used for fishing the Atlantic from a boat.

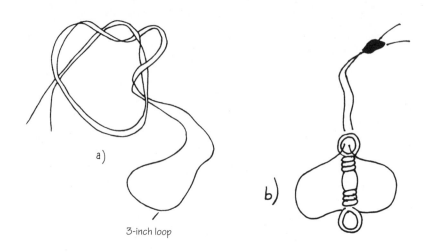

3-inch loop

Figure 3-4: Making the rig. (a) Find the loose end of the line and make a 3-inch loop by tying a double overhand knot about 18 inches from the end. (b) Pass this loop through the eye of a swivel and then around the swivel. Tie the #2 hook on the remaining end using the Fisherman's knot. Now tie a 5-inch loop 12 inches below the first knot, again using a double overhand knot. Place a 4 oz pyramid weight on this loop by passing the loop through the eye of the weight and then around the weight (as with the swivel in b). Trim the remaining end to be 12 inches long and use a Fisherman's knot to tie on a 1/0 hook.

Trolling

Trolling is another fishing alternative that is popular in the local Atlantic waters. With this fishing technique, baits and/or lures are dragged behind a boat slowly making way. Favorite catches of the trolling fisherman include king mackerel, Spanish mackerel, wahoo, dolphin, bonito, and others.

The advantages of the trolling technique include covering a lot of ground and giving the bait/lure forward motion, making it look more natural. Disadvantages of trolling include increased gas consumption, noise from the engines, and the need for a full-time helmsman.

The type of tackle used can be either of the types shown in Figure 1-3 or Figure 3-2 depending on how much of a fight you want to have on your hands. There are many different types of trolling lures and rigs used in the local waters. One of the most productive rigs is shown in Figure 3-6. This rig can be purchased ready to use or can be made by the fisherman. To make this rig, you will need a #5 swivel, a #5 snap swivel, a feather duster lure (red/white and blue/white lures are effective), some 60 lb test, steel, uncoated leader material, a bead-chain hook, some short lengths of copper wire, and a good pair of wire cutters.

First cut a length of leader material the length of the largest fish you expect to catch (48 to 60 inches is a good rule of thumb for trolling). Feed one end of the leader material through the eye of the snap swivel and tie an overhand knot as shown in Figure 2-4(a). Then, being careful to make a sharp 90 degree bend in the leader material, wrap the leader material

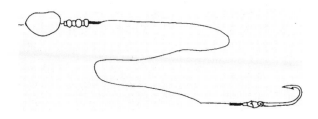

Figure 3-5: Large slip-rig used for fishing deeper water.

around itself in a barrel twist five to seven times. It is critical that the material be wrapped at a 90 degree angle as shown in Figure 2-4(b).

Now slide the leader material through hole in the feather duster's head and attach the black swivel (not a snap swivel) to the other end of the leader material using the same overhand knot followed by a barrel roll.

Once you have your rig, tie it onto the line using the Fisherman's knot. You are now ready to bait the bead-chain hook and attach it to the rig. You want the ballyhoo to look as natural as possible, so make sure it is completely thawed and gently move the body from side to side as if the fish were swimming to make the fish more flexible. Break off the beak of the ballyhoo close to its mouth leaving about 1/2" of the beak remaining.

Now it's time to attach the ballyhoo to the bead-chain hook. To do this, you will need a small wire threader like that shown in Figure 3-7. The threader will be used just like a sewing needle to get the bead-chain through the ballyhoo. Place the end of the bead-chain into the eye of the threader and then insert the threader into the anus of the ballyhoo as shown in Figure 3-8(a). Feed the threader through the ballyhoo and out the mouth of the ballyhoo. Now pull the threader and the end of the bead-chain out of the ballyhoo's mouth until the hook is secured as shown in Figure 3-8(b). Don't pull the bead-chain too far or you will bend the ballyhoo and it will spin while you are trolling, giving your bait an unnatural appearance.

Now take a short piece of copper wire and tightly wrap the bead-chain securely to the beak of the ballyhoo as shown in Figure 3-8(c). This copper wire will prevent the trolling motion from pulling the bead-chain and hook further through the ballyhoo, which would again bend the ballyhoo and cause unnatural spinning. Now that you have the ballyhoo on the bead-chain hook, attach the eye of the beak-chain to the snap swivel on the leader and you are ready to troll.

Check the drag setting of the reel to ensure that line will be fed out long before the breaking point of the line is reached but with enough tension to allow you to set the hook. Most fish caught using this technique will break the line if the drag is set too tight.

As the boat makes way at 2 or 3 knots (speed is not that critical), dip the baited feather duster into the water just beside the boat for a few seconds and watch how it trails against the boat's motion. It is critical that you make sure the rig is not spinning. You will limit your chances of catching a fish if your bait is spinning, since this doesn't look very natural. Common causes of spinning baits are partially frozen (i.e., bent) ballyhoo or improper attachment of the ballyhoo to the bead-chain hook. Check these things and if it is still spinning, try gently slapping the rig against the surface of the water a few times or switching ballyhoo.

Once the bait is trailing correctly, feed it out 30 to 50 yards behind the boat (the distance you let it out is not critical). Double-check the drag setting of the reel, place the rod in the rod holder, and begin your trolling. When trolling with multiple rods, be sure and put the lines out at different distances to help prevent them from getting entangled. Also, make wide

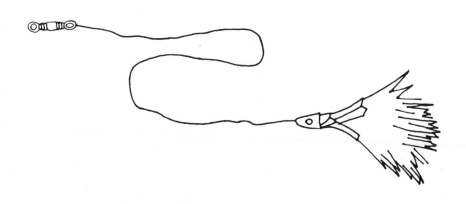

Figure 3-6: Rig used for trolling in the Atlantic.

gradual turns when trolling to avoid tangles. You may also want to use a plainer which allows you to troll a line deeper than normal. Since fish may be hanging at any depth on any given day, trolling a deep line or two may pay off.

Check the lines frequently to ensure that the baits are intact and that there is no seaweed on the line. When a fish hits a trolling line, the reel will sing out. When this happens, quickly pick up the rod, begin to wind the reel and snatch the rod tip up towards the sky several times. Since the fish should already be hooked, there is no need to wait before setting the hook as with other fishing techniques. Continue to hold tension in the line at all times by keeping the rod tip up and winding the reel to remove any slack that develops. If the fish is running and pulling out line against your drag, let him go. This is what you want to happen. The fish is working very hard and will soon tire. Once the running stops, wind the reel as you slowly lower the tip of the rod towards the fish being careful not to give any slack in the line. When the rod tip is pointed almost directly towards the fish, stop reeling and pull the rod tip gently back towards the sky. Continue this pumping action (reeling the tip down and then pulling the tip back towards the sky) to work the fish towards you. Let the fish get fully exhausted and under your control before trying to land him. After the fish is completely exhausted, hand-line or gaff the fish as necessary.

Figure 3-7: Tool (threader) used to pull chain through ballyhoo.

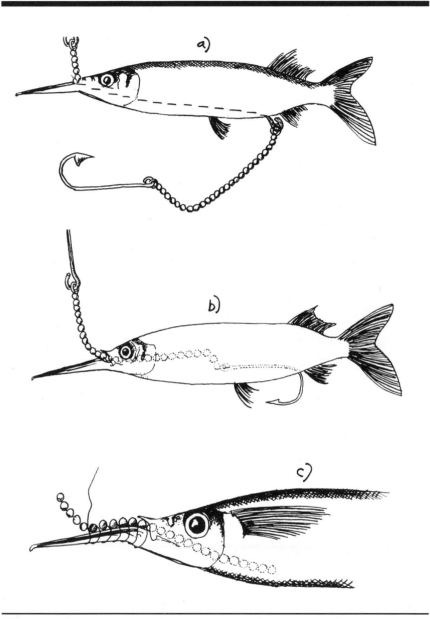

Figure 3-8 (a): Insert the threader into the anus of the ballyhoo. (b): Properly positioned bead chain. (c): Secure the remaining beak of the ballyhoo to the bead chain with a copper wire.

Drift Fishing

Drift fishing is a popular method of fishing the Atlantic waters from a boat. This technique is commonly used by charter boats and often yields king mackerel and dolphin among other species.

The rig used is shown in Figure 3-9. It consists of a length of steel leader material as long as the fish you intend to catch, a swivel used to tie the fishing line on and reduce line twisting, and three hooks linked together into a chain. Since you are usually fishing in the neighborhood of larger fish when drift fishing, use 60 lb test non-coated steel leader material just like that described in earlier under "Balloon Fishing" in Chapter 2. This leader material will be tough enough for the fish you are likely to catch and is easy to work with. A #5 black swivel is an appropriate size swivel and can't be easily seen by the fish. You will need three 4/0 or 5/0 single hooks with open eyes. These open-eyed hooks are stocked in most area tackle shops.

First, slide the barb of one hook through the eye of another as shown in Figure 3-10 and then bend the eye shut with a pair of pliers to link the three hooks securely together. Now you are ready to work with the leader material. You will need a pair of sharp wire cutters to cleanly cut the leader material. First cut a length of leader material the length of the largest fish you expect to catch (36 to 48 inches is a good rule of thumb). Attach the hook chain to the leader material using the barrel twist shown in Figure 2-4. Attach the swivel to the other end of the leader, again using the barrel twist.

After you have your drift fishing rig constructed, thread about a 1 oz egg weight onto your fishing line and then tie your fishing line to the swivel using the fisherman's knot. Now you are ready to bait your rig.

The most common bait used when drift fishing is dead sardines though most any small bait fish will do. Frozen sardines are readily available from local bait shops and work fine. To bait the drift fishing rig, start by threading the last hook through the tail of the bait fish. Then thread the second and finally the third hook into the bait fish. Your baited rig should look like Figure 3-11.

As the name implies, the boat is freely drifting with the wind and current when you are drift fishing. Most fishermen will position their boat up current from an underwater structure or reef. Then the fishermen will drop their drift fishing rigs down about 3/4 of the way to the bottom to prevent getting snagged on the underwater structure. Since most fish caught while drift fishing can easily break your line, make sure your drag is set below the breaking point of your line. Now you wait as the boat slowly drifts over the structure. If you get a hit, you will feel a very strong tug on your rod. Immediately begin reeling as you firmly snatch the rod tip towards the sky several times. Fight the fish as you would any other, allowing it to run at will and tire itself. You will likely need a boat gaff and gloves to bring the fish into the boat. The many LORAN coordinates provided later in this chapter will help you find underwater structures that lend themselves to drift fishing techniques.

Where to Go

When preparing to troll in the Atlantic waters, you can get many different answers to the question "Where is the best place to go?" Some fisherman will stop just outside the inlet or just any old place in the Atlantic and start fishing. Others will run ten miles or further off shore before putting out their lines. On any given day, either approach might be the correct one. Since the fish you normally catch trolling are always on the move, you are liable to catch fish anywhere in the Atlantic you might find yourself. This fact alone makes trolling a popular alternative for the fishermen not equipped with a fathometer and LORAN. Some things that can improve your trolling luck include fishing over and around free-floating weed lines, near the artificial reefs, listed later in this chapter, or around buoys. Since all of these attract small bait fish, they also attract larger fish that feed on the bait fish.

For those bottom fishing and drift fishing, finding a good reef is vital and

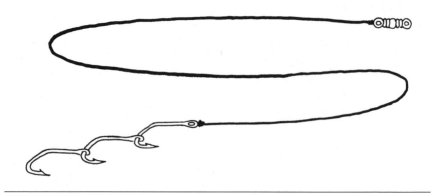

Figure 3-9: Rig commonly used for drift fishing in the Atlantic from a boat.

can make the difference between catching your limit or going home empty handed. Organisms grow on the reefs, providing food for smaller fish. As these smaller fish accumulate, the larger fish come to feed on them. A natural food chain is developed around the reef, providing for good bottom fishing and drift fishing. Since most of the Atlantic bottom

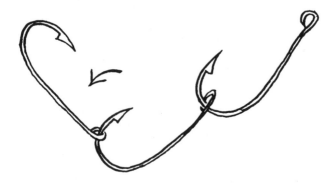

Figure 3-10: Open-eyed hook chain.

around the reefs is barren sand, the distance of a dozen yards can make all the difference in the world.

There are many reefs within reach of the properly equipped boater that consistently provide good fishing. Some of these spots are artificial reefs; others are natural rock ledges and coral reefs. Artificial reefs might consist of ships, airplanes, or the concrete rubble from an old bridge. Usually, these items are intentionally dumped into the Atlantic at pre-defined locations just to make reefs, which are good for the environment and good for fishing and SCUBA diving.

Navigational equipment is most helpful in finding these reefs. Ideally, you should be equipped with a LORAN and a fathometer. The LORAN, which stands for Long Range Aid to Navigation, tracks radio signals from land based LORAN stations and triangulates your position quite accurately. The fathometer maps the profile of the bottom as your vessel moves over it allowing you to pinpoint irregularities (such as reefs). For those equipped with a LORAN and a fathometer, Figure 3-14 gives the LORAN coordinates for many popular fishing spots.

Those without electronics can plot the LORAN coordinates on a chart that shows LORAN coordinates and then approximate compass head-

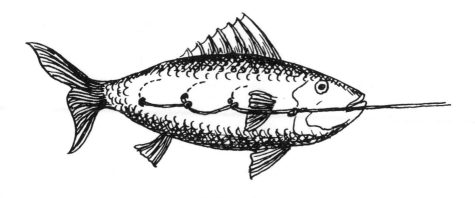

Figure 3-11: Hooking drift fishing bait.

ings and distances from area inlets to the fishing reefs. As new artificial reefs are built off shore, they are also marked with buoys for a period of time. Check the most current navigational charts to see what buoys are still maintained. On weekends or holidays when the weather is nice, the most popular spots may be populated with a number of fishing boats. If you anchor near the cluster of boats, you should be on or near enough to a reef to catch fish if they are biting. However, when using this approach, you should have a back up plan in case you can't find a crowd. Finally, there is another alternative to the boater without electronics. Another local book called *Diving Location* — published by McAllister Marine, 4850 N. E. 28 Ave., Lighthouse Point, Florida 33064, (305) 426-0808 — provides photos of land ranges that can be used to find some Gold Coast reefs that are close to shore. While its focus is on helping divers find diving locations, good diving locations usually make good fishing locations.

Fishing Charters

For those who don't have a boat, various types of charters are available that will allow you to catch fish in the Atlantic under the tutelage of experienced captains. There are basically two types of fishing charter boats: party boats and charter boats.

Party boats offer drift fishing exclusively. They typically take from 10 to 50 people on a boat for half day trips (about $35 per person) or full day trips (about $45 per person). Your party can consist of any number from one to a boatful. In either case, make reservations in advance to secure your spot on the boat. The captains of these boats go to many of the popular bottom fishing spots as well as their private spots, which are carefully guarded trade secrets. They usually offer a nice day on the Atlantic and good drift fishing for a fair price.

Charter boats also offer half day or full day trips. These types of charters are more tailored to your individual desires, as your party is the only group on board. They offer trolling (for everything from king mackerel to sailfish) as well as bottom fishing and drift fishing plus more individualized assistance. A typical price for this type of charter is $500 on a full day trip with an additional $45/person beyond six. A typical half day trip will run $250.

LORAN Coordinates to Popular Atlantic Fishing Locations

Name	Depth in feet	LORAN 14xxx	LORAN 62xxx	Latitude degrees/ minutes	Longitude degrees/ minutes
Esso Bonaire	90	14351.3	62006.5	26 56.79	79 59.61
Ms Jenny/Playpen	65	14351.4	62006.3	26 56.70	79 59.56
Jupiter Ledge	66/76	14348.4	62013.1	26 55.54	80 00.43
Juno Ledge	84/72	14341.3	62020.0	26 51.23	80 00.30
Zoo	100/75	14377.2	62020.1	26 48.19	79 59.32
Condos/100' Cave	100	14336.8	62020.7	26 47.98	79 59.36
Callaway's Ledge	93/106	14336.6	62021.0	26 47.87	79 59.38
Black Rock	92/107	14336.4	62020.9	26 47.71	79 59.31
Barge, 3rd Gully	60/73	14334.3	62025.5	26 46.81	79 59.89
Undercut Ledge	72/65	14333.8	62025.8	26 46.48	79 59.84
Amaryllis	75/60	14333.1	62027.5	26 46.24	80 00.13
Simpson's Bar	75/80	14333.2	62026.8	26 46.18	79 59.94
Mizpah & PC	83/60	14332.9	62027.8	26 46.11	80 00.10
Colson's Barge	75/68	14332.8	62026.3	26 45.97	79 59.79

Charts on pages 65-70 reprinted courtesy of McAllister Marine

Name	Depth in feet	LORAN 14xxx	LORAN 62xxx	Latitude degrees/ minutes	Longitude degrees/ minutes
New Reef	90/80	14331.2	62028.1	26 44.88	79 59.76
Eidsvag/Triangle	60/83	14331.1	62028.6	26 44.88	79 59.86
Rockpile	60/42	14330.4	62031.7	26 44.82	80 00.43
Boulders	80/85	14330.4	62029.2	26 44.45	79 59.83
Drifting Spot	75/90	14330.0	62029.3	26 44.17	79 59.76
Anchoring Spot	70/85	14329.7	62030.1	26 44.06	79 59.88
S Double Ledge	90/78	14328.5	62031.6	26 43.39	79 59.95
King Neptune	65/50	14327.3	62035.4	26 43.07	80 00.57
Breakers Shallow	20/30	14325.4	62039.0	26 42.20	80 00.98
Lopata's Ledge	70/55	14325.6	62035.1	26 41.76	80 00.09
4th Window	55/66	14325.2	62035.4	26 41.50	80 00.07
Breakers South	50/60	14324.5	62036.5	26 41.15	80 00.17
Flower Gardens	68/53	14323.7	62037.0	26 40.63	80 00.10
Bath & Tennis	43/55	14322.6	62038.7	26 40.07	80 00.24
Outfall Trench	60/50	14324.7	62026.0	26 41.22	80 00.09
Roccapriore's Ledge	50/55	14321.9	62039.4	26 39.65	80 00.25
Jeanine's Ravine	47/55	14321.8	62039.6	26 39.61	80 00.27
Sloan's Curve	51/63	14321.5	62039.5	26 39.44	80 00.20
Paul's Reef	45/55	14319.2	62042.7	26 38.15	80 00.41
PB Horseshoe	45/60	14316.2	62045.9	26 36.41	80 00.64

Name	Depth in feet	LORAN 14xxx	LORAN 62xxx	Latitude degrees/ minutes	Longitude degrees/ minutes
Trabits Ledge	58/68	14316.2	62045.8	26 36.39	80 00.45
Fay's Reef	50/40	14315.0	62047.5	26 35.66	80 00.51
Lady Anne Reef	45/52	14314.0	62048.7	26 35.21	80 00.64
Big Brain Coral	60/50	14312.3	62050.3	26 34.20	80 00.63
Tindell's Reef	45/55	14311.7	62051.1	26 33.88	80 00.69
Drift Fishing Paradise	65/55	14310.6	62052.6	26 33.29	80 00.80
Lynn's Reef	45/60	14305.1	62059.2	26 30.26	80 01.14
Boynton Ledge Cave	48/65	14304.9	62059.4	26 30.14	80 01.15
Tumbled Rocks	65/48	14302.9	62051.9	26 29.06	80 01.30
Tongue of Reef	61/48	14302.1	62063.3	26 28.69	80 01.46
Boynton Ledge	65	14301.6	62063.9	26 28.42	80 01.50
"Budweiser Bar"	95/75	14300.5	62064.9	26 27.76	80 01.49
Genesis Reef	87	14300.3	62065.4	26 27.73	80 01.62
Boynton Ledge Comb	55/70	14300.0	62064.7	26 27.36	80 01.33

Latitude and longitude numbers below and on the following pages are based on the Global Positioning System (GPS)					
Tumbled Rocks	53/65	14302.9	62061.9	26 30.12	80 02.23
Boynton Ledge	65/50	14301.6	62063.9	26 29.41	80 02.33

Name	Depth in feet	LORAN 14xxx	LORAN 62xxx	Latitude degrees/ minutes	Longitude degrees/ minutes
Boynton Ledge Comb	70/55	14300.0	62064.7	26 29.13	80 02.37
Delray Snapper Hole	50/65	14298.6	62068.0	26 28.75	80 02.31
"Budweiser Bar"	95/75	14300.5	62064.9	26 28.74	80 02.32
Genesis	86/74	14300.3	62065.4	26 28.73	80 02.29
Seagate Grouper Hole	50/65	14297.4	62069.9	26 27.91	80 02.79
Fink's Grouper Hole	51/70	14292.8	62065.3	26 24.67	80 03.09
Boca North Beach Ledge	60/50	14287.9	62080.6	26 21.93	80 03.29
Boca Third Reef Ledge	65/55	14287.1	62081.4	26 21.51	80 03.33
Lone Pine	30/33+	14286.3	62984.1	26 21.45	80 03.60
Boca Outfall Trench	70/50	14286.3	62082.2	26 21.02	80 03.32
Boca Artifical Reef Ledge	68/53	14283.8	62085.2	26 19.68	80 03.55
"Noula Express"	55-81	14283.3	62085.4	26 19.29	80 03.46
Deerfield Field Debris	66/73	14282.8	62087.4	26 18.94	80 03.75
Separated Rocks	42/37	14281.8	62088.9	26 18.78	80 03.98
Hillsboro Ledge	35/42	14280.5	62090.5	26 18.33	80 04.06
"Ancient Mariner"	45/68	14281.1	62088.6	26 18.11	80 03.70
"Berry Patch"	65/55	14281.1	62088.4	26 18.09	80 03.71

Name	Depth in feet	LORAN 14xxx	LORAN 62xxx	Latitude degrees/ minutes	Longitude degrees/ minutes
Cannon's Mound, North	35/43	14279.8	62091.2	26 17.61	80 04.11
Cannon's Mound, South	35/43	14279.7	62091.4	26 17.57	80 04.15
Hillsboro Domes	35/45	14279.3	62091.7	26 17.37	80 04.10
Hillsboro Outside Edge	60/45	14279.0	62090.6	26 16.95	80 03.77
"Abby Too"	55/45	14278.0	62091.6	26 16.43	80 03.84
The Horseshoe	33/45	14277.5	62093.5	26 16.35	80 04.20
Suzanne's Ledge	13/16	14273.6	62099.6	26 14.49	80 04.89
Steve's Landward Ledge	33/45	14273.2	62098.5	26 14.11	80 04.52
Steve's Seaward Ledge	35/45	14273.2	62098.4	26 14.03	80 04.56
Qualmann Tuggs et al	53/80	14273.7	62096.1	26 13.89	80 04.04
Rodeo 25th Anniversary Reef	43/120	14273.8	62095.3	26 13.88	80 03.81
Pompano 3rd Reef Ledge	55/65	14272.9	62097.4	26 13.70	80 04.17
RSB-1 ("Jim Torgerson")	5/500	14274.1	62095.0	26 13.64	80 03.95
Pompano Dropoff	12/30	14271.9	62101.3	26 13.60	80 04.97
"Captain Dan"	110/65	14272.3	62096.9	26 13.14	80 03.96

Name	Depth in feet	LORAN 14xxx	LORAN 62xxx	Latitude degrees/ minutes	Longitude degrees/ minutes
"Copenhagen"	12/30	14269.7	62103.7	26 12.30	80 05.00
The Sinkhole	60/94	14269.6	62101.3	26 11.87	80 04.46
Mark's Ledge	50/60	14269.8	62100.3	26 11.79	80 04.23
Anglin Pier Reef	46/57	14269.1	62101.3	26 11.47	80 04.35
Wreck of the "Rebel"	84/102	14267.0	62102.9	26 10.28	80 04.39
"Jay Scutti"	52/64	14265.2	62106.1	26 09.52	80 04.76
"Mercedes"	60/97	14265.3	62105.1	26 09.37	80 04.51
Oakland Ridges	22/43	14264.1	62109.2	26 09.22	80 05.30
"Robert Edmister"	55/67	14265.0	62107.0	26 09.16	80 04.84
Watkins Hole	67/75	14263.7	62106.9	26 08.55	80 04.64
The Houseboat	75/86	14263.8	62106.9	26 08.54	80 04.61
Hog Heaven	55/73	14262.6	62108.7	26 08.05	80 04.85
Marriott Airplane	65/72	14261.5	62109.9	26 07.43	80 04.93
Yankee Clipper Erojacks	6/15	14259.1	62115.5	26 06.67	80 05.87
Spotfin Reef	50/60	14258.6	62112.7	26 05.85	80 05.02
Spotfin Reefs/ Valleys	56/65	14258.7	62112.3	26 04.31	80 05.74
'Cuda Reef	25/35	14255.2	62118.2	26 04.30	80 05.73
Dania Pier Erojacks	11/20	14253.5	62121.9	26 03.76	80 06.40
Tenneco Platforms	78/103	14246.9	62122.4	25 58.95	80 05.01

Chapter

4

Local Fish Recipes

The abundance and variety of local fish species have made seafood a staple along the Gold Coast. Over the years, Floridians have experimented with literally thousands of different recipes for preparing freshly caught fish. This chapter provides some of their favorite recipes.

Fried Fish Pieces

5 pounds fish fillets	1 teaspoon salt
1½ cups milk	½ teaspoon pepper
½ cup Kellogg's corn flake	1 teaspoon Lawry's
crumbs	seasoned salt
1 cup flour	Peanut oil

Skin and fillet fish. Cut into bite-sized pieces. Put fish into a small bowl and cover with milk; refrigerate for 1 hour.

In a bowl mix corn flake crumbs, flour, salt, pepper and Lawry's salt. Roll fish in flour mixture. Fry fish in deep fryer at 400 degrees until brown, 3–5 minutes. Fry 8–10 pieces at a time, keeping oil very hot.

Yield: 10 servings

Broiled Fish

4 fish fillets (snapper,
    scampi, Spanish mackerel)
4 tablespoons butter
4 tablespoons lemon juice

4 teaspoons prepared
    mustard
Parmesan cheese
Paprika

Preheat oven to 350 degrees. Line a shallow baking dish with aluminum foil. Place fish fillets, skin side down, in baking dish. In a saucepan, melt butter. Stir in lemon juice and mustard. Pour over fish fillets. Bake for 10–20 minutes, depending on thickness of fillets. Baste several times with sauce. Sprinkle with Parmesan cheese and paprika, and broil until brown and bubbly.

Yield: 4 servings

Easy and Delicious Fish

Fish fillets
Lemon juice
Salt and pepper

Mayonnaise
Parmesan cheese
Paprika

Preheat oven to 450 degrees. Wash fish and pat dry. Line a baking dish with foil. Place fish skin side down in baking dish. Squeeze lemon juice over fish; sprinkle generously with salt and pepper. Spread mayonnaise evenly over fish, including the edges. Sprinkle with Parmesan cheese and paprika. Bake for 15–20 minutes, or until done. Run under broiler for 1 minute or until lightly browned and puffed.

Yield: ½ pound fish per person

Flounder Florentine

2 10-ounce packages
  frozen chopped
  spinach
2 tablespoons butter
¼ cup finely chopped
  onion
2 cloves garlic, pressed
½ teaspoon salt
¼ teaspoon pepper
¼ teaspoon freshly grated
  nutmeg
2 tablespoons butter
2 tablespoons flour

½ cup half and half
½ cup fish stock
10 flounder fillets,
  skinned
⅓ cup lemon juice
2 teaspoons Worcestershire
  sauce
½ cup butter
2 cups finely chopped
  mushrooms
2 tablespoons flour
1 cup sour cream
½ cup Parmesan cheese

Cook spinach according to package directions. Drain well. Set aside. In a heavy skillet, melt 2 tablespoons butter and sauté onion and garlic. Add drained spinach, salt, pepper and nutmeg. Simmer 4 minutes.

In a heavy saucepan, melt 2 tablespoons butter over medium-high heat. Add flour and cook, stirring constantly, until mixture is bubbling. Add half and half and fish stock. Continue stirring until sauce is thick and smooth. Add white sauce to spinach mixture and stir well. Remove from heat.

Preheat oven to 400 degrees. Place a spoonful of spinach mixture on each flounder fillet. Roll up and place seam-side down in a buttered baking dish. In a small saucepan, melt ½ cup butter. Add Worcestershire sauce and lemon juice; pour over fillets. Cover baking dish with foil and bake for 20 minutes.

Pour liquid from fish into a skillet and sauté mushrooms until most of the liquid is reduced. Remove from heat. Combine flour and sour cream; gently stir into mushrooms. Pour over fish and sprinkle with cheese. Brown fish lightly under broiler.

Yield: 8 servings

Redfish

2 or 3 pounds redfish	1 tablespoon dry white
Salt and pepper	wine
1 pound butter	Parmesan cheese
Lemon juice	Paprika

Preheat oven to 400 degrees. Fillet fish and sprinkle with salt and pepper. Put butter into shallow baking pan in hot oven until it is browned. Place fillets flesh side down in sizzling hot butter and return pan to oven for 10–15 minutes. Turn fillets with spatula and baste with pan juices. Sprinkle each piece with lemon juice, wine, cheese and paprika. Return to oven until done, about 5 minutes. Then broil for 1 minute. Baste fish with sauce.

Yield: 4 servings (This recipe works well for any fish fillet)

Polynesian Fish Dish

3 pounds snapper, scamp,	½ teaspoon marjoram
or any similar fish, cut	½ can cream of shrimp
into fillets	soup
⅓ cup lime juice	½ cup sour cream
¼ cup butter, melted	3 green onions and tops,
½ teaspoon salt	thinly sliced
¼ teaspoon pepper	½ cup tiny boiled shrimp

Wash fish and pat dry. Place in oven-proof, shallow baking dish, pour lime juice over fish and marinate 15 minutes. Pour off lime juice and pour melted butter over fish. Sprinkle with salt, pepper and marjoram. Broil 10 minutes; baste with pan juices. Cool slightly. Mix soup and sour cream; spoon some over each piece of fish. Garnish with onion and shrimp. Bake in a preheated 350 degree oven until thoroughly heated.

Yield: 6 servings

Red Snapper with Sour Cream Dressing

½ cup chopped onion
1 cup chopped celery
½ cup butter, melted
½ cup dry bread crumbs
½ cup sour cream
¼ cup lemon, peeled and
   diced

3 pounds red snapper
   fillets
Lemon juice
Salt
Paprika
Chopped parsley

Preheat oven to 350 degrees. Combine onion, celery, butter, bread crumbs, sour cream and lemon. Spread mixture in a greased baking dish. Place fillets on top and season with lemon juice, salt, paprika and parsley. Bake for 30–40 minutes, depending on thickness of fillets. Fish is done when it flakes, but is not dry.

Yield: 6 servings

Trout Amandine

1½ cup half and half
3 eggs
1 teaspoon salt
½ teaspoon white pepper
3 pounds fresh speckled
   trout, filleted and skinned

Flour
Vegetable oil for frying
2 cups sliced almonds
1 cup butter
Lemon wedges

Make a batter of half and half, eggs, salt, and white pepper. Dredge fish in flour; dip into batter and then into flour again. Fry in hot oil until golden brown. Drain on paper towels. Sauté almonds in butter until golden brown. Serve fish topped with almonds and garnished with a wedge of lemon.

Yield: 6 servings

Red Snapper Veracruz Style

3 pounds fresh
   Snapper fillets
2 tablespoons fresh lime
   juice
1 teaspoon salt

Flour
Salt and pepper
Vegetable oil for frying
3 tablespoons olive oil

Sprinkle fish with lime juice and salt; set aside for two hours. While fish marinates, prepare sauce.

Sauce: ¼ cup olive oil
   1 medium onion, thinly
      sliced
   2 large cloves garlic,
      peeled and sliced
   2 pounds fresh tomatoes,
      peeled, seeded and
      chopped

1 large bay leaf
   ¼ teaspoon oregano
   12 pitted green olives,
      halved
   2 tablespoons capers
   2 pickled jalapeños, cut
      into strips
   Salt

Heat oil and cook onion and garlic until tender but not brown. Add remaining ingredients and simmer about 30 minutes.

Preheat oven to 325 degrees. Dredge fish in flour, seasoned with salt and pepper, and fry in hot oil until golden brown. Place in a large baking dish or in individual baking dishes and top with sauce. Sprinkle top of sauce with olive oil and bake uncovered about 20 minutes or until just tender.

This can also be done with a whole 3-pound snapper. Cook 30 minutes.

Yield: 6–8 servings

Grilled King Mackerel Steaks

2 pounds fresh or frozen king mackerel steaks	2 tablespoons chopped parsley
¼ cup orange juice	1 tablespoon lemon juice
¼ cup soy sauce	½ teaspoon pepper
2 tablespoons ketchup	1 clove garlic, crushed
2 tablespoons oil	½ teaspoon oregano

Thaw frozen steaks. Cut into serving-size portions and place single layer in shallow baking dish. Combine remaining ingredients to make sauce and pour over fish. Let stand for 30 minutes, turning once. Remove fish, reserving sauce for basting. Place fish in well-greased, hinged wire grills. Cook about 4 inches from moderately hot coals for 8 minutes. Baste with sauce. Turn and cook 7–10 minutes longer, or until fish flakes easily when tested with a fork.

Yield: 6 servings

These recipes as well as many others (from soups to desserts) are published in The Junior League of Pensacola's cookbook, *SOME LIKE IT SOUTH!* Proceeds from the sale of *SOME LIKE IT SOUTH!* are returned to the community through the programs and projects of The Junior League of Pensacola, Inc.

Appendix A:
Fish Identification Charts

This appendix will help you identifiy what you catch. While compre-
hensive coverage of the many fish in the Atlantic and adjacent waters
is beyond the scope of this book, some of the most popular and
common fish are included here.

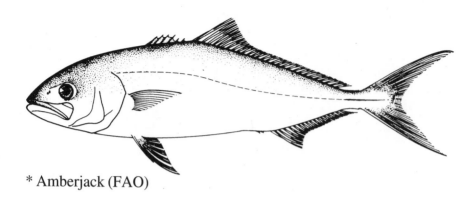

* Amberjack (FAO)

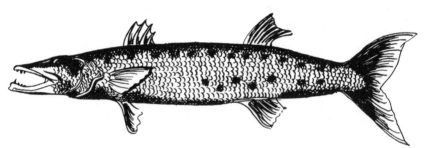

* Great Barracuda (Langan)

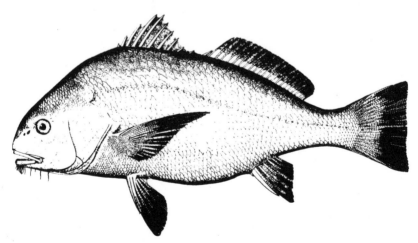

* Black Drum (Smithsonian)

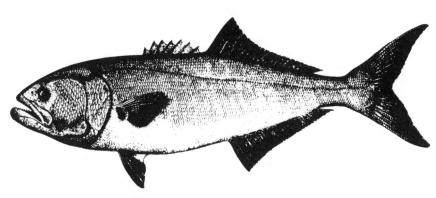

* Bluefish (Smithsonian)

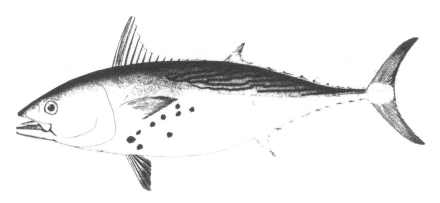

* Atlantic Bonito (Smithsonian)

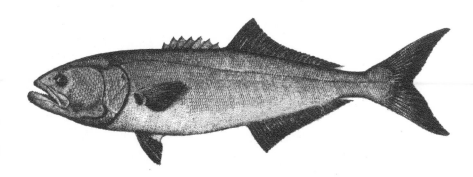

* Cero Mackerel (Smithsonian)

* Cobia (Smithsonian)

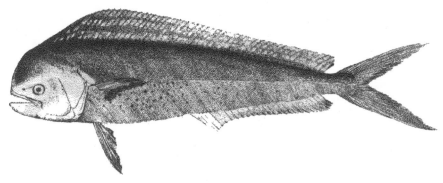

* Dolphin (Smithsonian)

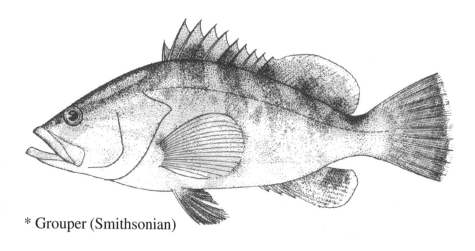

* Grouper (Smithsonian)

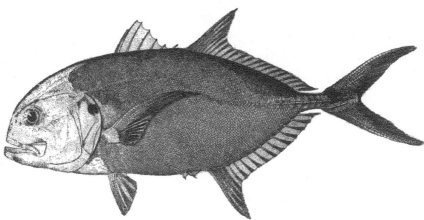

* Jack Crevalle (Smithsonian)

* King Mackerel (Smithsonian)

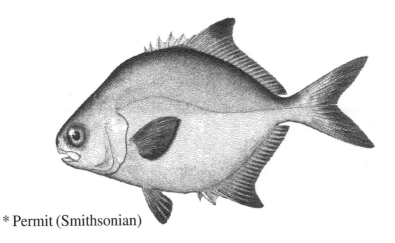

* Permit (Smithsonian)

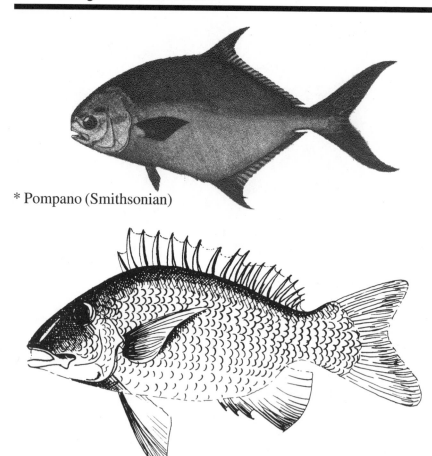

* Pompano (Smithsonian)

* Red Snapper (Langan)

* Sheepshead (Smithsonian)

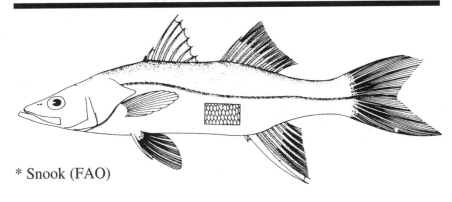

* Snook (FAO)

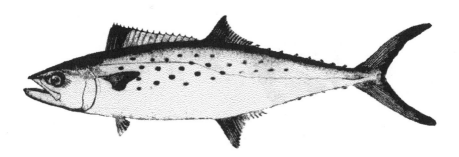

* Spanish Mackerel (Smithsonian)

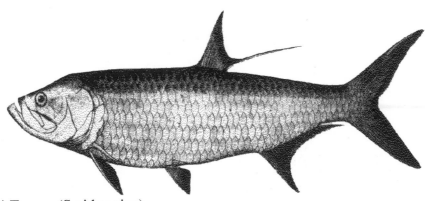

* Tarpon (Smithsonian)

* Trigger fish (Smithsonian)

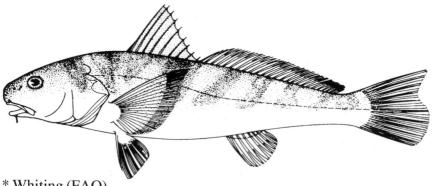

* Whiting (FAO)

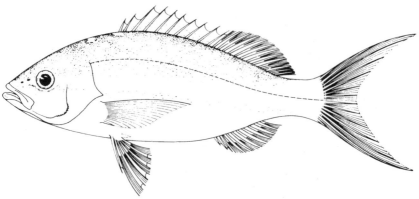

* Yellow tail Snapper (FAO)

Appendix B: Area Maps

This appendix will help you find the fishing spots described in Chapters 1 and 2. There are three maps included:

* Palm Beach County
* Broward County
* Dade County

The fishing spots discussed in Chapters 1 and 2 are marked on these maps.

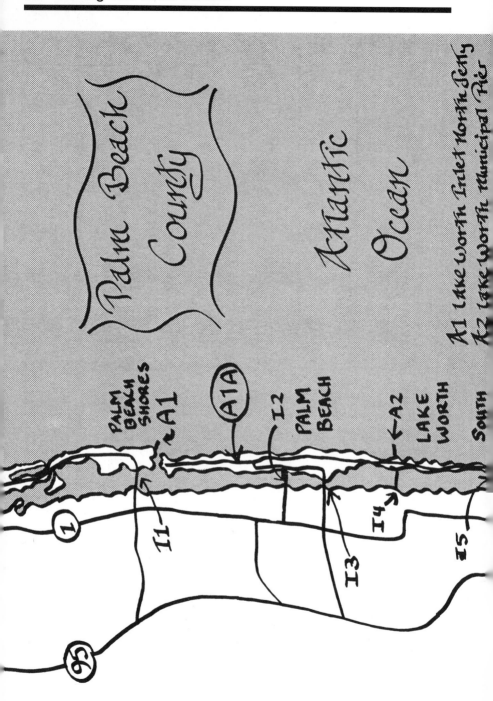

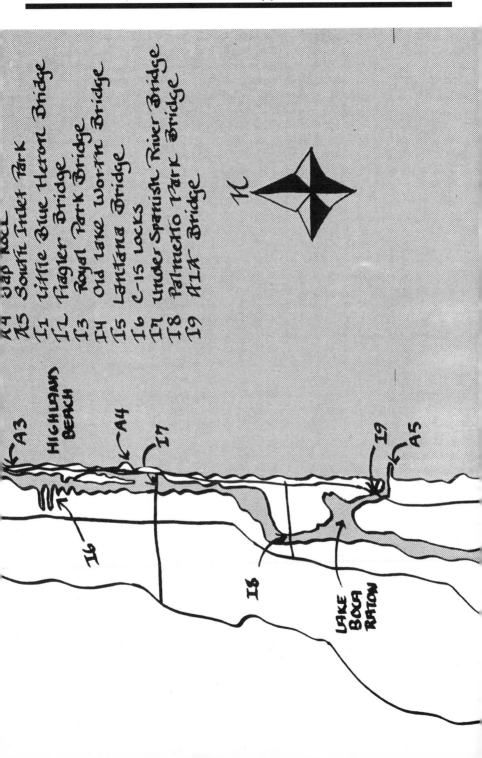

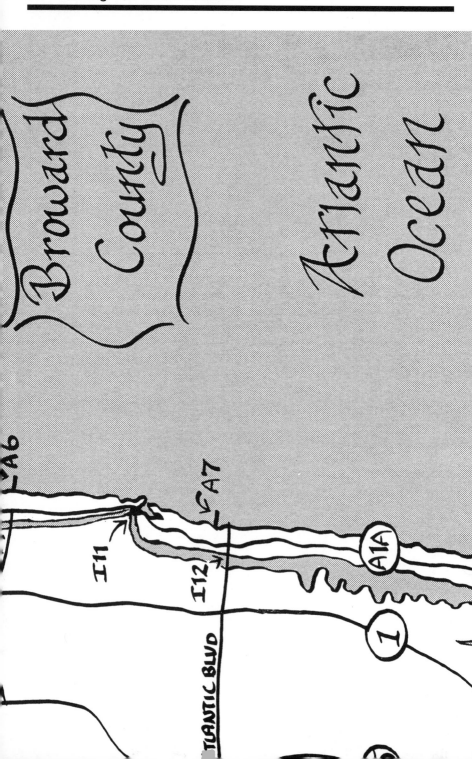

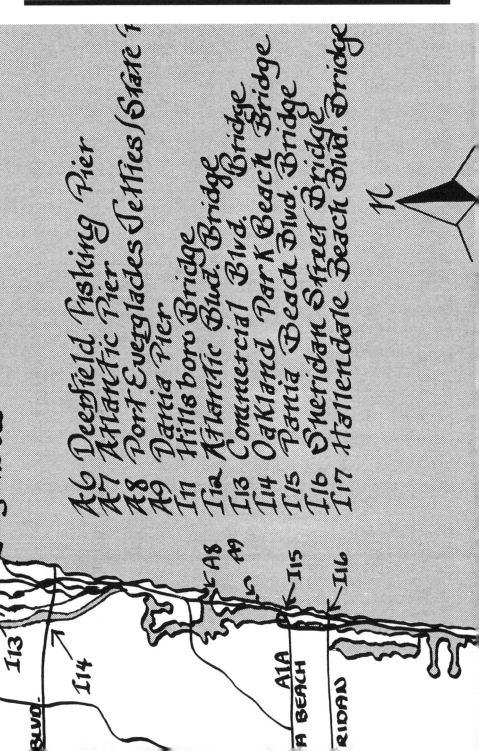

A6 Deerfield Fishing Pier
A7 Atlantic Pier
A8 Port Everglades Jetties/State 7
A9 Dania Pier
I11 Hillsboro Bridge
I12 Atlantic Blvd. Bridge
I13 Commercial Blvd. Bridge
I14 Oakland Park Beach Bridge
I15 Dania Beach Blvd. Bridge
I16 Sheridan Street Bridge
I17 Hallendale Beach Blvd. Bridge

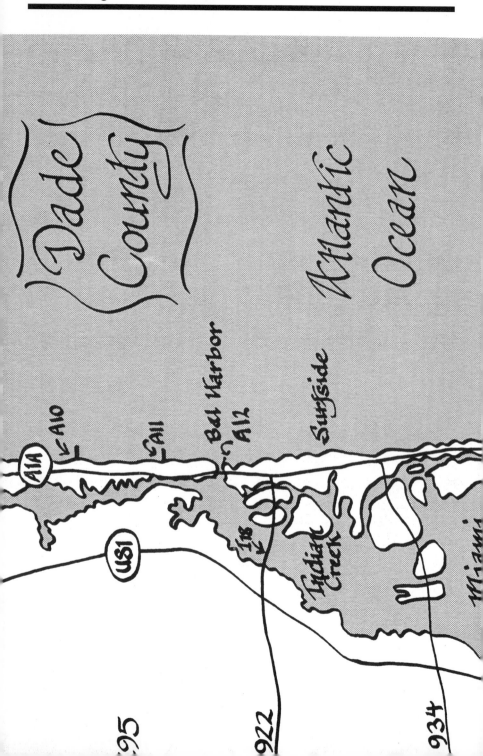

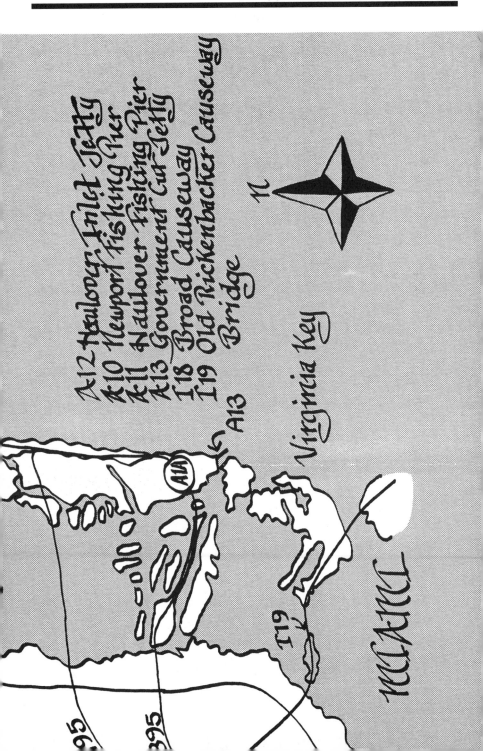

The Fisherman's Directory

A guide to local businesses that cater to fisherman

North Palm Beach

Juno Bait & Tackle 407-694-2797

Riviera Beach

Bob Schneider
   Custom Lures 407-845-1994
Murray Bros. 407-845-1043
Salt Water Sportsman
   Tournament Office ... 407-863-1433

West Palm Beach

Dave's Purple Worm
   Bait & Tackle 407-684-0913
Kleiser's Sport Shop 407-655-4434
The Corner Store 407-832-2452
The Corner Store 407-655-3046

Loxahatchee

Loxahatchee Bait
   & Tackle 407-793-6558

Lake Worth

Classic Bassin'
   Pro Shop 407-967-2248

Lantana

Perk's Bait &
   Tackle Shop 407-582-3133

Boynton Beach

Boynton Fisherman's
   Supply 407-736-0568
Boynton Inlet Bait
   & Tackle 407-737-3997

Boca Raton

Boca Marine 407-392-0243
Gold Coast Custom
   Tackle Co. 407-394-6497

Deerfield

A-Walker's Bait
  & Tackle No 407-426-2061

Lighthouse Point

Custom Rod &
  Gun Inc. 407-781-5600

Coral Springs

The Bait Bucket 407-755-3291

Pompano/Coral Springs

A-Bob's Offshore
  Shop Bait 407-782-2888
A-Walker's Bait
  & Tackle Shop 407-946-1040
Abe's Bait & Tackle 407-978-3502
Bait Busters
  Tackle Inc. 407-942-3474
Fish N Stuff 407-942-3923
Fisherman's One Stop .. 407-946-1307
Fisherman's Wharf
  of Pompano Beach 407-943-1488
Hillsboro Rod & Reel ... 407-946-9023
Miller's Fishing
  Supply 407-781-4651
Pompano Beach
  Fishing Rodeo 407-942-4513

Margate

Denny's Bass Shop 407-968-7751
Margate Tackle Box 407-974-0921

Southern Bass & Offshore
  Tackle Shop 407-979-4933

Coconut Creek

Sawgrass Bait &
  Tackle 407-973-9555

Lauderdale-by-the-Sea

Anglin's Fishing Pier ... 407-491-9403
T&R Tackle Shop 407-776-1055

North Lauderdale

One For The Wall
  Taxidermy 407-222-9286

Oakland Park

Del's Bait & Tackle 407-492-1194

Ft. Lauderdale

84 Bait & Tackle 305-473-4684
Bahia Mar Marine
  Store 305-764-8831
Bassmen's Bait
  & Tackle 305-581-1985
Beach Bait & Tackle 305-764-1141
Bill Boyd's Bait
  & Tackle 305-462-8366
Carl's Bait &
  Tackle Shop 305-581-8890
Charlie's Bait
  & Tackle 305-764-6603
Ken Cote Rod Builder .. 305-491-6025

Ft. Lauderdale
(continued)

Custom Rod
& Marine 305-523-5330
Everglades Holiday
Park 305-434-8111
Fly Shop 305-722-5822
Herman's World
of Sporting 305-522-4499
Kingsbury & Sons
Tackle & Gun Shop .. 305-467-3474
Les Will's Bait Tackle
& Gun Shop 305-583-7302
LMR Custom Rods
& Tackle 305-525-2592
Lou's Tackle & Marina 305-989-9219
McIntosh Marine Inc. .. 305-764-1211
Roy's Bait & Tackle 305-527-6670
Tournament Angler 305-492-9794

Plantation

BJ's Bait & Tackle 305-475-0248
Bluebills Bait Tackle
& Gun 305-472-6467

Dania

Angler's Tackle Shop ... 305-922-6484
Laurino Custom
Fishing Rods 305-925-7706

Davie

Competition Tackle
& Marine 305-581-4476

Davie
(continued)

Everglades Pro-Bass
Center 305-434-4495
Hinkle Bait & Tackle ... 305-583-2189

Hollywood

Jim's Going Fishing 305-963-2499

North Miami Beach

Herman's World
of Sporting 305-944-1166
J&J Bait & Tackle 305-945-5554
Ocean Marine 305-949-1333

North Miami

Historic Blue Marlin
Fisher 305-949-9004
The House of Snook 305-891-8062

Hialeah

Fisherman's Hut 305-769-9878
Genesis Fishing
Supply 305-362-6654
Herman's World
of Sporting 305-887-3929
Iggie's Fishing &
Tackle 305-887-3929
J&J Sports 305-557-9869
Outdoor Sports
Headquarters 305-822-2640
Powerline Marine 305-557-3551

Hialeah Gardens

Leeward Rod Co. 305-823-7857

Miami Springs

Aquarius Fishing Rod
& Tackle 305-885-1312

Miami Beach

Junior's Tackle Shop
of Miami 305-672-3089

Miami

B&F Marine Inc. 305-634-3807
Better Bait
   Supply Inc. 305-358-0277
Burt's Place 305-233-0848
C&A Gun &
   Tackle Shop 305-687-6313
Canal Bait & Tackle 305-261-8939
Captain Harry's Fishing
   Supply 305-374-4661
Caribbean
   Hatcheries Inc. 305-247-7877
Crook & Crook
   Marine Supplies 305-854-0005
Dade Corners 305-553-6203
Dawson Marine
   Service 305-374-0208
El Captain
   Sports Center 305-635-7500
El Serrucho 305-262-6181
Fish Headquarters 305-757-5817
Fishing Line, The 305-598-2444

Fisherman's Paradise ... 305-634-1578
Fisherman's Paradise ... 305-232-6000
Fred Lou Tackle 305-949-5515
Fresh Tackle &
   Marine Supply 305-381-8494
Gordon's Bait & Tackle 305-444-4344
Haulover Park
   Fishing Pier 305-947-6767
Herman's World
   of Sporting 407-732-9000
Herman's World
   of Sporting 305-979-9000
Herman's World
   of Sporting 305-966-5771
Herman's World
   of Sporting 305-749-1166
Herman's World
   of Sporting 305-270-0011
Herman's World
   of Sporting 407-732-9000
Herman's World
   of Sporting 305-238-1166
Herman's World
   of Sporting 305-232-1794
Hi-Lo Food Store
   Bait & Tackle 305-444-7101
Hnos Gomez Bait
   & Tackle 305-444-7101
Jet's Florida Outdoors .. 305-221-1371
Kendall Bait &
   Tackle Inc 305-666-6600
Marinsa Miami Corp ... 305-252-0118
Ned's Bait & Tackle 305-226-2185
Phil's Bait & Tackle 305-251-1443
RJ Marine & Tackle
   Supplies 305-232-4378
Reef Tackle Shop 305-757-4373

Miami
(continued)

Reel Fishin' Tackle 305-284-8106
River Marine
    Supply Inc. 305-856-0080
Sea Shack 305-279-8285
South Bay
    Marine Store 305-859-2124
Star Rods 305-592-3134
Tony's Outdoor Sporting
    Goods 305-279-8068
Universal Tackle Corp . 305-634-1591
Vic's Rod &
    Reel Repair 305-371-2378
Weber-King Bait Farm 305-233-2282
Williams Bait
    & Tackle 305-255-6118
World Wide
    Sportsman Inc 305-238-9252

Tavernier

Tavernier Creek
    Marina 305-252-0194

Key Biscayne

Chief's Bait &
    Tackle Inc 305-361-1499

Homestead

Fishing Rod Components
    of S 305-245-6422
Plantation Fisheries 305-248-4043

Index

A

air pumps
  diving 17

B

barrel twist 52
bottom fishing 27, 35, 46

C

cast fishing 27
charter boat 56

D

diver down flag 43
double drop 27
drag 32
drift fishing 27, 56

E

no entries

F

Fisherman's knot
  knots 16
free spool 32

G

gaff 83, 27, 45

H

hand-line   46
hook
  multi-pronged   13
  single   28
  single barb   13

I

inland waters   11

J

no entries

K

no entries

L

LORAN coordinates   65
lures   34, 51
  duster   51

M

mullet   13, 27, 28

N

no entries

O

no entries

P

no entries

Q

no entries

R

no entries

S

shrimp   13, 27, 28
steel leader   28, 29
swivel   13, 28

T

trolling   50

U

no entries

V

no entries

W

weight
  egg   13, 27
  pyramid   28

X

no entries

Y

no entries

Z

no entries